Jira Quick Start Guide

Manage your projects efficiently using the all-new Jira

Ravi Sagar

BIRMINGHAM - MUMBAI

Jira Quick Start Guide

Commissioning Editor: Richa Tripathi
Acquisition Editor: Aditi Gour
Content Development Editor: Smit Carvalho
Technical Editor: Akhil Nair
Copy Editor: Safis Editing
Project Coordinator: Pragati Shukla
Proofreader: Safis Editing
Indexer: Manju Arasan
Graphics: Jason Monteiro
Production Coordinator: Nilesh Mohite

First published: January 2019

Production reference: 1230119

Published by Packt Publishing Ltd.
Livery Place
35 Livery Street
Birmingham
B3 2PB, UK.

ISBN 978-1-78934-267-3

www.packtpub.com

I would like to dedicate this book to my wife, Shelly, who has always stood by me and helped me achieve my goals. This book wouldn't have been possible without her continuous encouragement. I would also want to dedicate this book to my little daughter, Raavya, my parents for their endless support and to all the reviewers and book coordinators for their immense help on this book.

`mapt.io`

Mapt is an online digital library that gives you full access to over 5,000 books and videos, as well as industry leading tools to help you plan your personal development and advance your career. For more information, please visit our website.

Why subscribe?

- Spend less time learning and more time coding with practical eBooks and Videos from over 4,000 industry professionals

- Improve your learning with Skill Plans built especially for you

- Get a free eBook or video every month

- Mapt is fully searchable

- Copy and paste, print, and bookmark content

Packt.com

Did you know that Packt offers eBook versions of every book published, with PDF and ePub files available? You can upgrade to the eBook version at `www.packt.com` and as a print book customer, you are entitled to a discount on the eBook copy. Get in touch with us at `customercare@packtpub.com` for more details.

At `www.packt.com`, you can also read a collection of free technical articles, sign up for a range of free newsletters, and receive exclusive discounts and offers on Packt books and eBooks.

Contributors

About the author

Ravi Sagar is an Atlassian consultant and Drupal expert with several years of experience in web development and business analysis. He has done extensive work implementing and customizing big Jira instances for project tracking, test management, support tickets, and Agile tracking.

Ravi founded Sparxsys Solutions Pvt. Ltd. in 2010—a start-up company that provides consultancy and training services on Atlassian tools and Drupal. He has a keen interest in building accessible websites, adhering to WCAG guidelines, and is the author of *Mastering Jira 7 - Second Edition* and multiple Jira 7 video training courses. In his free time, he loves blogging on his website, where he writes regularly about topics such as DevOps and programming.

About the reviewer

Raul Pelaez Mendoza is an Atlassian Jira Expert based in Barcelona with more than 7 years of experience in the Atlassian Ecosystem and more than 20 years of experience in the implementation of Java-based systems for project management offices in diverse public and private international corporations.

Specialist in business process outsourcing (BPO) and operations management. Currently working at Ankonan doing consulting services, training courses, and the administration of the Atlassian platforms of diverse companies.

Technical Engineer in Computer Systems, Technology Teacher Certificate, SNOMED-CT/HL7/CDA Certified. Specialist in Intellectual Property Expertise. IT-Forensics Expert. Certified Blockchain Solution Architect (CBSA).

Packt is searching for authors like you

If you're interested in becoming an author for Packt, please visit authors.packtpub.com and apply today. We have worked with thousands of developers and tech professionals, just like you, to help them share their insight with the global tech community. You can make a general application, apply for a specific hot topic that we are recruiting an author for, or submit your own idea.

Table of Contents

Preface

Jira Quick Start Guide is focused on getting you started with Jira very quickly, and is written specially with this objective in mind. Like any other tool, Jira also has a learning curve, but quite often, you don't want to spend weeks or even months just evaluating the product. This book will give you sufficient knowledge of using the tool not just as a user, but also as an administrator. The book starts by giving you a very good overview of Jira and how it can help you, then talks about Jira basics that will help you understand how it can be applied in your project. Later chapters are focused on exploring the customization capabilities of Jira to empower you with the knowledge of various schemes that cannot be ignored if you want to use Jira for your project.

Who this book is for

This book will be especially useful for project managers, but is also intended for other Jira users, including developers, and any other industry besides software development, who would like to leverage Jira's powerful task management and workflow features to better manage their business processes. We will cover how to configure projects and boards, customize workflows, and manage project permissions in Jira. This book provides a comprehensive explanation covering all major applications of Jira, including Jira Software, Jira Service Desk, and Jira Core. It will cover planning and setting up a new Jira instance. We will talk about key features such as understanding the basic usage of the tools, setting up workflows for processes, and other things such as reporting in Jira and an understanding of various best practices.

Primarily, the book is focused on project managers, developers, and service desk agents, as well as business users with, of course, good exposure to Jira administration concepts.

This book will cover all the aspects of using Jira for project management, service desk operation, and business processes.

What this book covers

Chapter 1, *Introducing Jira*, gives you a comprehensive overview of what Jira is as a tool, what problems it tries to solve, and various types of Jira applications.

Chapter 2, *Getting Started with Jira Core and Basic Usage,* will teach you how to set up Jira and start using it immediately. This chapter is focused on Jira Core for business teams and will focus on the basic usage of the tool.

Chapter 3, *Using Jira Software for Development Teams,* covers how Jira can be used for software development using agile-based projects. This chapter will show you how agile boards work in Jira.

Chapter 4, *Using Jira Service Desk for Helpdesk,* is focused primarily on using Jira Service Desk for your support desk. Here, we will cover various aspects of Jira Service Desk, including Portal, Queues, and SLAs.

Chapter 5, *Jira Schemes and Configuring Project Workflow,* starts the journey of Jira customization so you feel more empowered in using Jira in a way that suits you. This chapter will kick-start configuring your Jira instance by modifying the workflows.

Chapter 6, *Configuring Project Screens and Permissions,* continues the customization aspects of Jira. Here, we will show how to add new fields in your project, and also learn how to control who can do what in the project by looking at permissions.

Chapter 7, *Reports and Dashboards,* will show you how to analyze data in Jira by looking at the various reporting capabilities of the tool. We will look at project reports, as well as learn how to create our own custom dashboard.

Chapter 8, *Best Practices,* allows us to finally spend some time discussing various best practices that you should employ when using Jira in your organization. This will ensure top-notch performance of your Jira instance, and make sure that administration of your instance is not a daunting experience.

To get the most out of this book

- This book requires you to have access to a Jira instance. Since we will be using a cloud version of Jira, you don't even need to install anything. Just sign up for a Jira Cloud instance and start following the book.
- There are no prerequisites required to understand the Jira concepts mentioned in this book; however, a little awareness of agile and Service Desk, although not required, will help.
- This book is written with a wide range of readers in mind. As long as you have the desire to learn Jira, this book will definitely help you.

Conventions used

There are a number of text conventions used throughout this book.

`CodeInText`: Indicates code words in text, database table names, folder names, filenames, file extensions, pathnames, dummy URLs, user input, and Twitter handles. Here is an example: "Type in `boards`"

Bold: Indicates a new term, an important word, or words that you see onscreen. For example, words in menus or dialog boxes appear in the text like this. Here is an example: "In the Discover new products page then click on **Free trial** button right next to Jira Software"

Warnings or important notes appear like this.

Tips and tricks appear like this.

Get in touch

Feedback from our readers is always welcome.

General feedback: If you have questions about any aspect of this book, mention the book title in the subject of your message and email us at `customercare@packtpub.com`.

Errata: Although we have taken every care to ensure the accuracy of our content, mistakes do happen. If you have found a mistake in this book, we would be grateful if you would report this to us. Please visit `www.packt.com/submit-errata`, selecting your book, clicking on the Errata Submission Form link, and entering the details.

Piracy: If you come across any illegal copies of our works in any form on the Internet, we would be grateful if you would provide us with the location address or website name. Please contact us at `copyright@packt.com` with a link to the material.

If you are interested in becoming an author: If there is a topic that you have expertise in and you are interested in either writing or contributing to a book, please visit `authors.packtpub.com`.

Reviews

Please leave a review. Once you have read and used this book, why not leave a review on the site that you purchased it from? Potential readers can then see and use your unbiased opinion to make purchase decisions, we at Packt can understand what you think about our products, and our authors can see your feedback on their book. Thank you!

For more information about Packt, please visit packt.com.

Introducing Jira

1

In this chapter, we'll understand what Jira is and how it can be used as an issue tracking tool by various teams in an organization. It's one of the most popular tools developed by Atlassian, which is the company behind it. Jira comes in three different flavors and, in this chapter, we'll also discuss the differences between these three flavors.

We'll go through what problems Jira solves, the benefits and main features that set Jira apart from other tools, and finally we'll spend time understanding Jira Core, Jira Software, and Jira Service Desk by going through the unique features that are available in these three applications.

Finally, we'll share which application you should use for your requirements in the organization.

The following topics will be covered in this chapter:

- What is Jira?
- Jira Core
- Jira Software
- Jira Service Desk
- The problems Jira solves
- What are the main benefits of Jira?
- How to decide which application to use
- Deployment options

What is Jira?

Jira is a proprietary issue-tracking system. It can be used to track bugs, resolve issues, and manage project functions. There are many tools available on the market, but the best thing about Jira is that it can be easily customized and configured to suit the specific needs of an organisation and there are plenty of ways to add more features.

Out-of-the-box, Jira offers defect/bug tracking functionalities, but it can also be customized to act like a help desk system, a simple test management suite, or a project management system with end-to-end traceability for software development projects.

Jira is mainly accessed using a web browser but it has lot of integrations with other tools and Jira comes with a RESTful API so you can interact with it programmatically.

Jira Core

Jira Core is one of the basic flavors of Jira and targets business teams that need a tool that's flexible, can be customized to their needs, and is easy to use as well.

Jira Core is perfectly suited for teams such as marketing, operations, HR, legal, and finance. It has all of the features of workflows, dashboards, and reports.

Jira Software

The target team for Jira Software—as the name suggests—is a team interested in using a tool that can help them implement Agile methodologies such as Scrum and Kanban.

Jira Software comes with standard features such as creating Agile boards for better transparency. There are features to plan, track, release, and report. It has all of the features of Jira Core so you can be assured that it's powerful enough when it comes to customization.

Jira Service Desk

Apart from business teams and software teams, Jira Service Desk targets support desks or help desks.

In Jira Service Desk, there are the standard features of a service desk tool such as a customer portal to raise tickets and search in the knowledge base for self-serve for customers; for the agents who will be handling the tickets, they have configurable queues. Just like Jira Software, Jira Service Desk also contains all of the features and benefits of Jira Core.

As you must have already guessed, Jira Core is the most basic tool and, based on your requirements and whether you want to develop software using Agile methodologies, the waterfall methodology, or a custom development process, you can use Jira Software. For providing support to your customers and handling tickets in Jira, you can use Jira Service Desk.

The problems Jira solves

Jira has become one of the most popular tools in the industry, by not just software development teams but also by people who are working on support desk and business teams. Jira essentially is an issue tracking tool, where issue is a generic term for a ticket that could be a task, bug, story, epic in software development projects, a simple to-do in business projects, or an incident, problem, or service request in service desk-based projects. The popularity of Jira increased because of the fact that it can be customized very easily for a variety of use cases.

Challenges and problems that Jira solves

We want to spend some time talking about various challenges and problems that are faced by teams or organizations in using various tools.

Lack of flexibility

There are lot of development methodologies in the industry that have become standard. These methodologies are used and adopted by many organizations. For instance, Agile methodologies such as Scrum and Kanban are one of the most widely used techniques but, let's be honest, irrespective of these standards, each company's way of working is different and there are many factors that changes the way a company works.

Scrum and Kanban methodologies provide a common framework and there are many tools that can help the easy adoption of these tools; however, a tool should be flexible enough to accommodate the needs of the team. A tool should adhere to standards but, at the same time, should be flexible enough to allow adjustments from the teams.

Difficulty in customization

Most of the methodologies that are adopted by teams for either development purposes or support are driven by a process, which is nothing but a life cycle with different stages. The most simple process can have just three stages, such as To do, In progress, and Done. When a new task is started it's usually waiting for someone to pick it up and when they have completed the task, they simple update the status of the task to Done.

Now, in most cases, the complexity of the process is defined by the type of activity (task or bug), what information needs to be captured (summary, description, and so one) while planning the work, the life cycle or the workflow of the task, and tracking the work using reports. Standards, such as Scrum/Kanban (Agile) or ITSM (Service Desk), provide a framework but the teams trying to adopt these industry standards still need a way to tweak the tool based on their requirements. Maybe they need to ensure that users or developers attach a file when they resolve a task or they want to send a notification to the developer when the task is assigned to them.

Any tool should allow such customization so the teams using it can fully benefit from it.

Difficulty in adoption by teams

Tools are used to solve a problem, not to over-complicate it. A freelancer working on a laptop building code might not need to rely on a tool to help them; a small team of a few developers can develop code by keeping track of their activities in a spreadsheet; and a small help desk team receiving a couple of tickets once in a while can also use and manage their work using emails only.

However, tools come into the picture when these teams need to improve their efficiency and aspire to become more productive. Any tool you use should be easy to adopt by all. It should be easy for the administrators to set up and implement, it should be easy for management to plan and track the work, and finally it should be easy for the developers to use.

Extensive training to learn the tool

As discussed previously, the adoption of the tool shouldn't be difficult and hence some effort is required to train the people involved in the usage of the tool. However, the training and how quickly the team can start using the tool are also very important and should be key criteria in choosing which tool you should be using.

Expensive

The tools used in organizations provide lots of value and have obvious benefits; however, a tool should justify its cost and maintenance. A tool may be flexible, provides lots of customization, and is easy to use by everyone but if it's too expensive to implement and set up, then it will be difficult for an organization to justify the benefit.

There are plenty of tools and application that are flexible but are either too difficult to customize or require lot of effort. Some tools are easy to customize but require lots of training and require special skill-sets. Jira tries to tackle these challenges by providing the right balance. Most of the customization can be done from the UI and that enables teams to quickly get started, while at the same time having peace of mind and confidence in the tool because a slight change in the process such as adding a new state in the workflow won't require a week.

What are the main benefits of Jira?

If you're wondering whether you should be using Jira or not, these benefits will help you decide. It's very important that we highlight them.

The various benefits of using Jira are as follows:

- Standard tool for teams of all sizes
- Simple licensing model
- Lightweight tool
- Low maintenance
- Easy to use and intuitive
- Increased productivity
- Better visibility
- Integration with other tools
- Marketplace apps
- A RESTful API for limitless possibilities
- Atlassian Community

Let's now discuss these features in detail.

Standard tool for teams of all sizes

When you install Jira for the very first time, you'll find out that it's extremely easy to get started with the tool. You can use various out-of-the-box templates to create a project. Irrespective of your team size, you always have this option to use an industry-standard tool. Even for a small team, the configurations that come with the out-of-the-box templates are well defined. Jira doesn't differentiate its features based on the team size; whether you're a small team or a big enterprise, the features that you get in the tool are the same. The way a small team of 10 developers work on an Agile board will be the same as a big team of 50 developers working on multiple Agile boards.

Having this consistency is great not only for administrators but also for team members as the knowledge they gain by working on a tool such as Jira is always going to help them as the team grows in the future.

Simple licensing model

Jira is proprietary software developed by Atlassian and you need to purchase the license to use it. The licensing is based on the number of users you have in the team who will be using the system, and it's very straightforward.

Let's say you have 15 developers, five managers, and two administrators then you would have, in total, 22 users using the system and to understand the license that you need to purchase, just check on the Atlassian website. In the case of 22 users, there's a slab of 25 users that you need to purchase.

You can go to the following link to check the license that you need to purchase:

```
https://www.atlassian.com/software/jira/pricing?tab=self-hosted
```

When you open this link, you'll be presented with a screen as shown in the following screenshot where you can choose the deployment type—**Cloud** or **Self-hosted**—and then, based on the number of users, the license cost will be displayed to you:

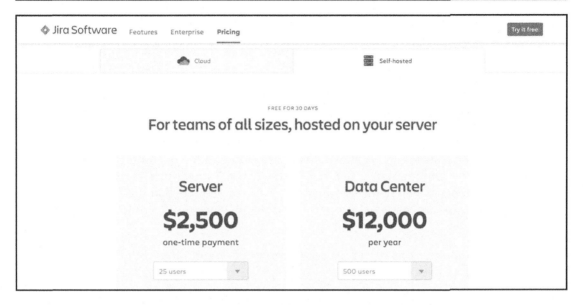

Figure 4

In the event the number of users increases in the future, additional licenses can always be purchased. It's advisable to keep in mind the expected usage of the tool in the next year at least. If, right now, there are 22 users but you know for a fact that this number will increase to 35 or 40, then it's better to buy licenses keeping in mind the future increase. This will save you some money, which isn't a bad idea at all.

There are various deployment options for using Jira that we'll discuss in this chapter but, to install Jira on your own server, you need to buy a license for a self-hosted deployment.

Lightweight tool

Installing Jira on your own server doesn't require heavy investment in infrastructure. It can run reasonably well on a server with 2 GB RAM and a multicore CPU; of course, it also depends on the size of the instance. For small instances with a few thousand issues to big instances with millions of issues, the server specifications can vary and that is the great part of using Jira.

Atlassian recommends some specifications on this page based on the size of the instance:

```
https://confluence.atlassian.com/adminjiraserver/jira-applications-
installation-requirements-938846826.html
```

If you're just getting started with a small instance then choose the specifications that are recommended by Atlassian in the preceding link. You aren't forced to set up a big infrastructure in the beginning.

Low maintenance

We discussed previously the challenges that you should be aware of when choosing the tool; apart from the features and cost, which are important in the beginning, you should also be aware of the running cost of the tool. Like any other tool, Jira also requires continuous maintenance where the administrator needs to ensure that the system is cleaned up regularly, backups are managed properly, and the instance itself is upgraded from time to time.

There are new minor versions of Jira released every other month that contains not only new features but also bug fixes.

Upgrading Jira and maintaining it are not at all a daunting task. With the right governance in place, it's quite simple to ensure good performance of the tool. Most Jira administrative actions are done from the UI and it's very convenient for the administrator to handle customizations and other recurring administrative tasks from the browser window.

Ease of use and intuitiveness

Using Jira is extremely intuitive and easy. Each user—whether a developer, manager, or administrator—will log in to Jira using a web browser. The moment they log in, they're presented with the Dashboard and depending upon the rights and permission of the user the appropriate features are shown and enabled for them.

Even though working on Jira is intuitive and doesn't require special training for the end user, there is, however, a learning curve. Most people who need to work on Jira learn by themselves but dedicated documentation is provided by Atlassian:

```
https://confluence.atlassian.com/alldoc/atlassian-documentation-32243719.html
```

The preceding link has the most up-to-date documentation of all of the Atlassian products including Jira Core, Jira Software, and Jira Service Desk.

Reading the documentation or a book like this one will help you quickly get started on the tool, and there are plenty of resources available to learn the tool to get the most out of it. However, if you're trying to roll out Jira in your company, then you can be assured that users can very quickly adopt it; with very short training or coaching sessions, it's very easy to introduce a tool such as Jira in your team.

Increased productivity

The ease of use and intuitiveness help a lot, as we just discussed in the preceding adoption of the tool section but when people start using Jira, you can then expect your productivity to increase. Not only is Jira a great tool for planning your activities or projects, but the day-to-day tracking is also very good in Jira. There are various ways through which your team is always up to date with the latest activities in the project. There are dashboards where everyone with the right access can see the information relevant to their team and themselves. Also, the tool has the capability to send notifications and reminders to users.

For example, users involved in a project or any task will get emails from the system. Of course, these email notifications can be customized to reduce noise but there are mechanisms to ensure that the overall team productivity is enhanced when using a tool such as Jira.

Better visibility

Planning and tracking activities are of no use when the team can't learn from their mistakes and improve upon them. There's a plethora of reports that we can create in Jira related to one or multiple projects.

In Jira, there's a concept of a dashboard where users, based on their permissions, can create one or multiple dashboards containing various gadgets to provide them with up-to-date reports.

These reports help the managers to not only stay on track but also to ensure that the overall progress is maintained and take appropriate action well before time. For instance, on the dashboard, we can see in graphical and tabular form the issues getting resolved versus closed issues in the past few months and a burndown chart, a pie chart to display the break-down of issues based on their workflow status.

The Agile boards that come with Jira Software always display the most up-to-date information to the whole team of developers and queues in Jira Service Desk also give agents an accurate picture of tickets in their backlog.

Bringing more visibility is one of the key points of Jira and it's really good at it.

Integration with other tools

Jira itself is a great tool; however, there are other tools from Atlassian, such as Confluence, which is used for online collaboration; Bitbucket for code repository; and Bamboo for continuous integration. Jira and most of the other tools from Atlassian talk to each other natively.

Atlassian has this ecosystem and set of integrated tools that can be used standalone but, when integrated with each other, provide a complete solution.

For example, if your organization is looking to implement DevOps practices using Atlassian tools, then you can use tools such as Bamboo, Bitbucket in conjunction with Confluence, and Jira integrated with most of them.

Apart from integrating with tools from Atlassian, Jira can also be integrated with third-party tools and that's done using either an app or an add-on, which we'll discuss in a moment, but for any other integration where you cannot find an app, there's also the possibility of using the Jira RESTful API.

Marketplace apps

Jira has lot of features out of the box and it comes with a few templates based on the type of application you use. For instance, when using Jira Software, you can create a project with either Scrum- or Kanban-based configurations. At the same time, you always have this option to modify and create your own set of configurations using various schemes in Jira. However, apart from the standard features in the tool and these customizations, if you need to extend the feature set of Jira, you can install various plugins better known as add-ons or more recently as apps.

These apps are either from Atlassian itself or from other companies—mostly Atlassian partners that have published these apps on the Marketplace:

```
https://marketplace.atlassian.com/
```

If you open this link, you'll be taken to the Atlassian Marketplace place where you can download thousands of apps for not only Jira but for all other Atlassian tools. As displayed in the following screenshot, you can either browse various apps or search for them:

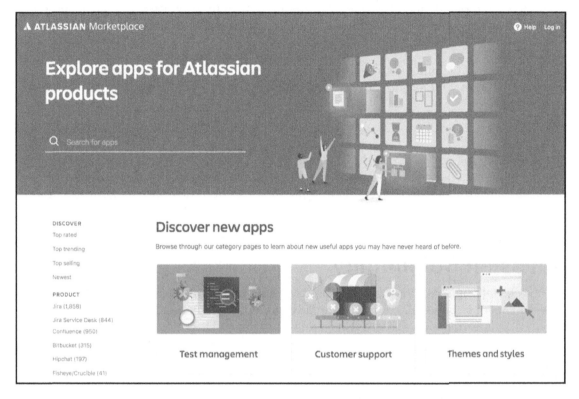

Figure 5

When you go to the Marketplace, you have the option to look at various popular apps for each Jira application but let's say you want to do **Test management** in Jira and you're wondering whether an app can quickly give you this option; you can download various apps from the Marketplace and evaluate them.

Having these apps gives you endless possibilities in Jira—of course, it depends on whether the app is good enough for your use case or not, but at least you know that, with the help of an app, you can do what you can't do out of the box. These apps either provide more functionality or provide integration with other tools.

A RESTful API for limitless possibilities

We just discussed the concept of an app that gives you more options in extending the features of the tool but, in case you are wondering how to programmatically push and pull data into Jira, then you'll be glad to know that Jira comes with a RESTful API, which is an amazing way to talk to Jira from other tools.

Whether you want to build your own interface, import data into Jira, or maybe interact with the tool from your existing legacy tool, then the RESTful API opens a lot of possibilities:

```
https://developer.atlassian.com/server/jira/platform/rest-apis/
```

The preceding link will give you the details of this amazing set of APIs in Jira. Most of the functionality that you access from the UI and various features can also be accessed using RESTful APIs. This enables developers to write their own interface and integrate with the tool.

Atlassian Community

We've been talking about the various benefits of Jira but this one requires special mention. Atlassian not only builds Jira, which is already quite popular in the industry, but it also provides a platform to have discussions about its tools:

```
https://community.atlassian.com/
```

Atlassian Community is one such platform where different types of users can come not only ask questions but also to share their knowledge and connect with other users. As shown in the following screenshot, the Atlassian Community home page will present you with an option to either click on a specific Atlassian product or search for the information you are looking for:

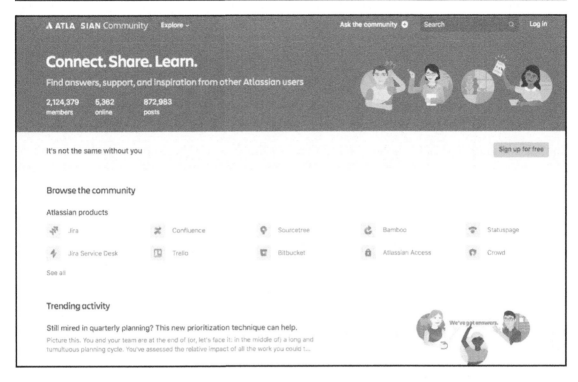

Figure 6

Let's say you have a question about a specific feature in Jira or you need some help with a specific topic, then you can come to this platform to ask your question and you'll surely get help from some other users on this platform.

Atlassian also continuously monitors this platform and gets regular feedback from the users and its customers. This helps them to improve their products.

How to decide which application to use?

Jira comes in three different flavors that we discussed briefly earlier. Now, if you're wondering whether you should be using Jira Core, Jira Software, or Jira Service Desk, then in this section we'll discuss how to choose which application is right for you.

Let's go through a high-level overview of these three applications:

- Jira Core is primarily Jira
- Jira Software is an application added to Jira Core; it provides Scrum and Kanban boards
- Jira Service Desk is an application added to Jira Core; it provides a customer portal, service requests, SLAs, and queues

The following table describes the potential uses of the three applications by various teams:

Jira Core	Jira Software	Jira Service Desk
Business teams that need a tool to plan and track their activities. Teams that can use Jira Core: marketing, operations, HR, legal, and finance. Any other team can use Jira Core.	Software development teams building and shipping software. Methodologies supported by Jira Software: SCRUM83 and Kanban. Jira Software supports typical Agile concepts along with standard Agile-based reports.	Service desks and IT support desks helping customer issues. It can be used to implement ITSM or ITIL. Key features include: customer portal, integration with Confluence for self-service, SLAs, and queues. Jira Service Desk doesn't put restrictions on the number of customers raising tickets.

The best part is that all three applications can be used together. You can have one Jira instance in your organization where a few teams can have their projects running on Jira Core without any Agile boards, the development team can have their projects with Jira Software, and the service desk team can have their project running on Jira Service Desk.

In most cases, it makes sense to have just one instance running all three applications, but these applications can be run on separate instances as well.

Deployment options

Primarily there are three ways to use Jira, each with its own benefits:

- Cloud
- Server
- Data Center

Cloud

To get started quickly, you can use the Cloud deployment option where you just need to sign up online and you can be up-and-running with your Jira instance within a few minutes. There's no installation required when using Cloud deployment. After signing up for Jira on the Cloud, just create your users. Your Jira instance can be accessed by a unique link that can be shared among your team.

- Atlassian sets up and hosts the instance
- There's no server, no storage, and no maintenance

Jira deployed on the Cloud can always be migrated to the server version; it also depends on what apps you're using and whether the app data supports the migration from Cloud to server.

Server

If you want to set up and install Jira on your own server running on premise, then you can download the Jira setup files and do the installation as per your needs. In terms of functionality, the server version of the application is more or less the same as the Cloud version:

- You set up and host the instance
- You manage the installation
- You maintain the instance

Jira installed on the Server can also be migrated to the cloud. An important thing to keep in mind is support for the app data.

Data Center

This is targeted at, and suitable for, big enterprise deployments of Jira. It's basically the Server version of Jira but installed on multiple nodes. The main benefits of Data Center deployment are high availability, disaster recovery, and scalability. This deployment is recommended if your organisation can't afford any downtime of Jira and it's mission-critical for your business.

Summary

In this chapter, we discussed what Jira is and how it can be used by organizations for various use cases. We spent time talking about the three different flavors of Jira: Jira Core, Jira Software, and Jira Service Desk; what problems these three applications solve; the benefits of using Jira; and various deployment options to kick-start your Jira journey.

Once you know about Jira, then it's time to start using the tool and in Chapter 2, *Getting Started with Jira and Basic Usage*, we'll first understand the importance of planning your Jira setup and then we'll sign up for a Jira Cloud instance to create a Jira Core project, understand various aspects of the project interface, and finally spend time going through the life cycle of an issue.

Getting Started with Jira Core and Basic Usage

2

In this chapter, we'll understand how to get start started with using Jira for your project. We'll start by spending time on planning our Jira installation by asking ourselves relevant questions. We'll set up a Jira cloud instance and a project of the Jira Core type. We'll, of course, start by understanding how to work on a project as a user and we'll cover various aspects of the project interface.

We'll also learn how a new project is created by a Jira Administrator and, as a project manager, how you can ensure that the scheme used in the project is correct and relevant for your requirements. We'll spend some time understanding how to create an issue, work on it, and close it.

Topics covered in this chapter include the following:

- Getting started with Jira
- Using Jira Core for business teams

Getting started with Jira

In this section, we'll set up a Jira instance that will be used for the rest of this book to learn various aspects of the tool; however, just like when using any tool, we need to ask ourselves some questions regarding its usage and that is why planning is a very important phase that we need to discuss first. We'll quickly set up a Jira instance on Atlassian Cloud to get started on our journey.

Planning your Jira installation

In the beginning, even before starting your journey with Jira, you need to think about your expectations of the tool and ask some questions. Let's discuss these questions that will help you make a wise decision about implementing Jira in your organization.

How many users will be using Jira?

Are you a team of 10 people that need a tool quickly to manage their day-to-day activity or do you work in a company of 10,000 employees, where a tool needs to be rolled our across your organization in several locations?

The number of existing users and the projected number of new users who might join your company need to be clear. This number is extremely important because, based on how many people want to have access to the tool, the right license needs to be bought. Jira licensing is quite straightforward and is based on the number of users. This number will help you in understanding how much Jira will cost you.

What problems are you trying to solve with Jira?

Jira has various advantages; in `Chapter 1`, *Introducing Jira*, we discussed in detail the benefits that Jira will bring, but whether you want to use Jira for your business or development teams and whatever processes you want to implement in Jira, such as Scrum or Kanban, need to be clear from the beginning.

Jira can be customized for different use cases such as Defect Tracking, Test Management, Change Management, Requirement Management, and Helpdesk. Based on these expectations, your choice of application will be different. More importantly, you should have convincing justification about the benefits that Jira will bring to improve your current efficiency and productivity in the team.

Which application and what apps would you need?

We just discussed that Jira can be customized for a variety of use cases and your expectations from these customizations will help you decide what Jira application you need.

Let's go through some examples of common requirements and possible solutions using the right application and app:

Your requirements	Application and apps you would need
For instance, if your Agile development team is currently struggling with managing their sprints and is looking for a tool for time sheet management.	Jira Software and Tempo Timesheets
Your legal team of four people currently uses a shared Excel sheet to keep track of all of the cases along with the person handling them and the current status of case.	Jira Core
You help desk team is currently receiving around 10-15 tickets from various customers everyday but it's getting difficult for them to effectively manage the support requests.	Jira Service Desk

Apart from using one of the applications individually, you can also have one instance of Jira running more than one application or all of them. Since these applications are licensed separately, it's better for you to spend time in the beginning identifying which applications you would need.

How many projects do you want to create in Jira?

When using Jira, there's no limit on the number of projects you can create; however, how many projects will use a specific type of application is important. For instance, your Jira instance can have the following scenarios:

- Two projects using Jira Core
- Ten projects using Jira Software
- One project using Jira Service Desk

In this scenario, you'll have a total of 13 projects but each project can have its own set of configurations that will define how the project will behave. Documenting possible use cases and configurations is invaluable for maintaining your instance. In the future, whenever a new project is created in Jira, it's advisable to use an existing set of configurations and follow a standard across your organization. The number of projects and the type of application it would need is important to also optimize the licenses.

Also, a higher number of projects would mean that there will be lot of issues in your instance and this can be key information in deciding on a deployment option as well; for example, if your Jira is to be used by thousands of users working on millions of issues or tickets, then data center deployment is what you would need.

What will be the projected usage in six months and one year from now?

We just discussed how the number of projects and users in your instances will help you decide on the type of applications and the deployment option, but if you also have plans to scale up the usage of the tool, then buying a sufficient number of licenses in the beginning of the deployment would actually save you more money than upgrading your license tier after six months.

So always do some projects about the projected usage of the tool in the next few years.

Integration with other tools

One of the best things about Jira is its ability to integrate with other tools, not just from Atlassian but from other third-party vendors as well.

Do you need to integrate with your active directory in the company or do you want Jira to integrate with Confluence, which is an online collaboration tool from Atlassian? Or is there a legacy tool in the company that needs to be pushing data into Jira? There are some integrations such as Jira with Bitbucket or Jira with Confluence that can happen out of the box, but for some integrations; you will need an app or a custom development. Answering these questions will help you decide early on about the apps that you need to buy from the market place or your approach towards using Jira with other tools using development.

Choosing a deployment

We discussed in detail various deployment options in `Chapter 1`, *Introducing Jira,* namely, Cloud, Server, and Data Center. To identify which option is more suitable and the best for you, answering the following questions will help you:

Questions	Answer	Suitable deployment
How quickly do you want to get started with Jira?	Immediately	Atlassian Cloud can get you started with Jira almost within minutes
Do you have the infrastructure and internal resources to manage the application?	Yes	Jira Server on your own premises
Will Jira be accessed from multiple locations?	No	Jira Server on your own premises
Will Jira be mission-critical for your business and can you afford downtime?	Yes	Jira Data Center
Do you need top-notch performance of your Jira instance?	Yes	Jira Data Center

Bear in mind that it's possible to move from the Cloud to the Server model and vice versa later on but it's still better if you answer these questions and evaluate the best deployment for your organization.

Setting up a Cloud instance

This book is a quick start guide on Jira and that's why we'll be using a Cloud instance of Jira till the end of this guide.

Follow these steps to sign up for Atlassian Jira Cloud:

1. Open the following link to evaluate Jira Core: `https://www.atlassian.com/software/jira/core/try`.
2. Click on the **Try it free** button at the bottom-left as shown in the following screenshot:

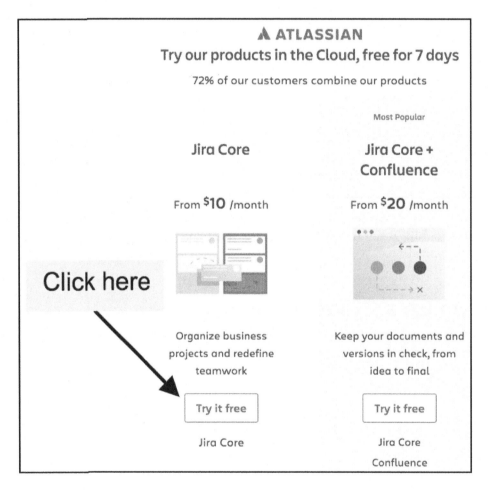

Figure 1: Evaluate Jira Core

3. On the new screen, sign up for an evaluation on Atlassian Cloud. Complete **Claim your site**, **Full name**, **Email**, and **Password** and click on the **Sign up** button.
4. Your Jira instance on Atlassian Cloud will then be set up for you.
5. On the next screen, select your preferred language and click on the **Continue** button.
6. On the next set of screens, you'll be asked to upload your avatar picture.

Congratulations, you now have a new Jira instance set up on Atlassian Cloud. You can evaluate this instance free of cost for one week. After that, you will need to buy the license. If you're evaluating Jira for the very first time, using the Atlassian Cloud version is a great way to get familiar with its features.

If you want to evaluate Jira further, then you can either purchase a starter license that will cost $10 per month for 10 users or you can evaluate Jira Server-on-premise for one month and then pay a $10 one-time fee for 10 users.

If you're purely evaluating Jira and you need more time, then you always sign up for a new account free of cost.

To learn about the core concepts of Jira please visit the following link: `https://hub.packtpub.com/jira-101/`

Using Jira Core for business teams

Great work, you have a Cloud instance of Jira ready. Now let's first get familiar with the basic features of the tool. Let's quickly create a project in Jira Core.

Creating a new project

Let's now create a new project in Jira:

1. On the **Welcome** screen, click on the **Create sample project** button, as shown in the following:

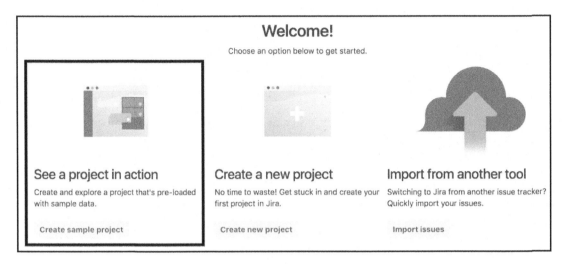

Figure 2

2. On the **Create project with sample data** screen, you'll be asked to select a template, which in this case would just be **Project management**, as we just have the Jira Core application in our instance. When we install Jira Software and Jira Service Desk, then more templates will appear in this screen. Click on the **Next** button:

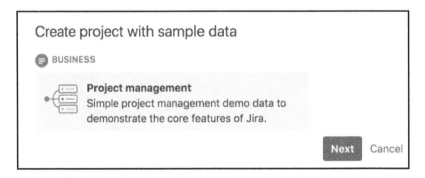

Figure 3

3. The next screen will ask you to provide some information. Enter the **Name** as **Human Resource**; the **Key** will automatically be set to **HR** but you can change it if you want; and **Project lead** will be your name but, when you add more people in your instance, you'll select their names. Finally, click on the **Submit** button to create the project.

4. Your first project will be created for you, similar to the one shown in the following screenshot:

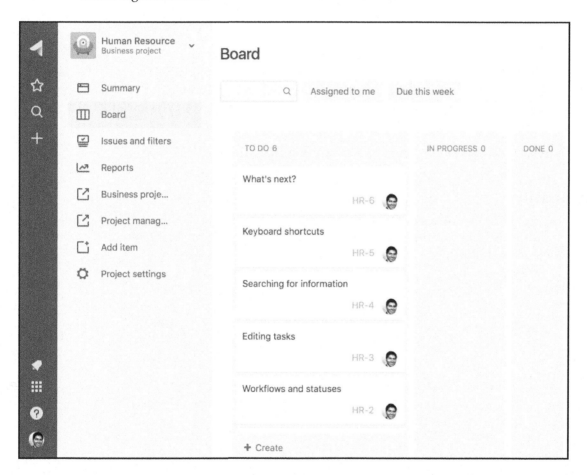

Figure 4

Let's now explore various features in a Jira Core project.

Working on a Jira Core project

We now have a new project called **Human Resource** in our Jira instance. Each project in Jira also has a Project Key, which in our case is **HR**. A project in Jira is a container of issues, which are just nothing but tickets or different activities.

The project sidebar shown on the left side of the project has links to sections related to the current project. In a Jira Core project, there are links to **Summary**, **Board**, **Issues and filters**, and **Reports.**

Summary

As you might have guessed already, this section contains a summary of what's happening in your project. The purpose of this section is to give you a bird's-eye view of what's happening in the project.

There are two tabs on this screen—**Activity** and **Statistics**.

Activity

A project in Jira is always evolving and things are changing in it. New issues are added to the project, people are adding comments on them, and issues are being resolved as well, as shown in the following:

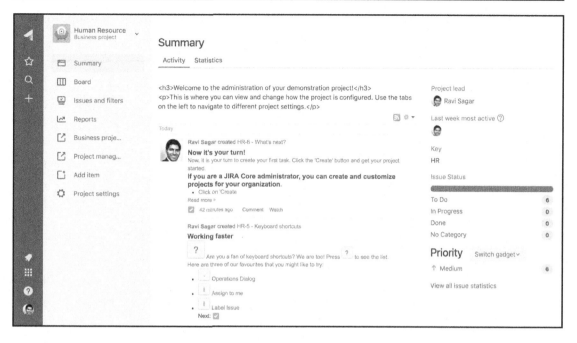

Figure 5

As you can see in the preceding screenshot, the latest comments are displayed in the center of the page and, on the right-hand side, there's information about the **Project lead**, a count of **Issue Status** per workflow status, and a similar count based on **Priority**.

Statistics

There are various fields in a Jira issue that help us identify problems better and plan them accordingly, such as **Priority**, **Status**, and **Component**.

This page will display a breakdown of issues with counts and percentages of issues for various issue attributes, as shown in the following screenshot:

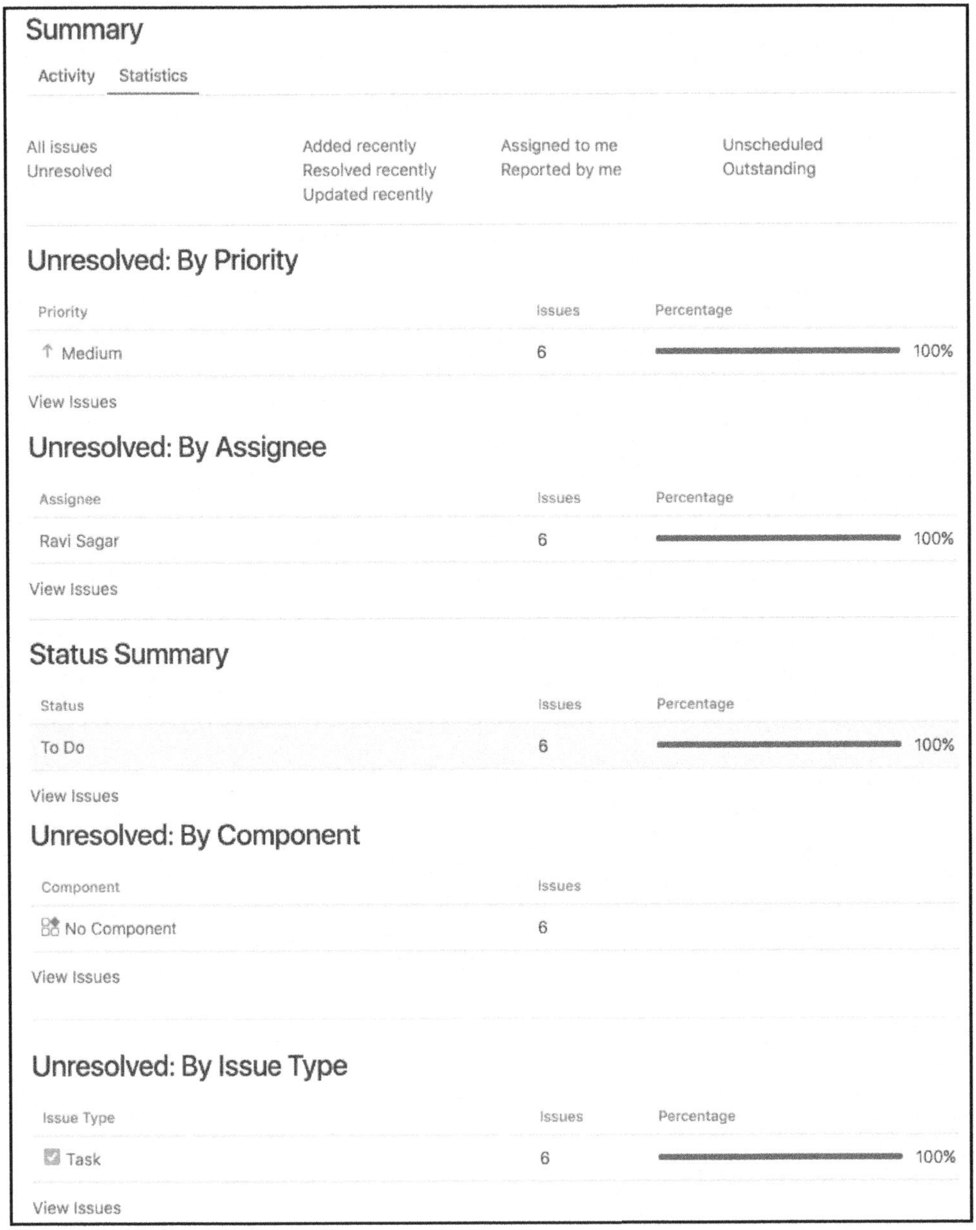

Summary

Activity   Statistics

All issues	Added recently	Assigned to me	Unscheduled
Unresolved	Resolved recently	Reported by me	Outstanding
	Updated recently		

Unresolved: By Priority

Priority	Issues	Percentage	
↑ Medium	6	▬▬▬▬▬▬▬▬▬▬▬	100%

View Issues

Unresolved: By Assignee

Assignee	Issues	Percentage	
Ravi Sagar	6	▬▬▬▬▬▬▬▬▬▬▬	100%

View Issues

Status Summary

Status	Issues	Percentage	
To Do	6	▬▬▬▬▬▬▬▬▬▬▬	100%

View Issues

Unresolved: By Component

Component	Issues
No Component	6

View Issues

Unresolved: By Issue Type

Issue Type	Issues	Percentage	
Task	6	▬▬▬▬▬▬▬▬▬▬▬	100%

View Issues

Figure 6

As more issues are added in the project, this section will become more useful with handy links to take you directly to a list of issues.

Board

This section has three columns—**To Do**, **In Progress**, and **Done**. It's a great way to visualize the work happening in the project. As people in the project start working, they can drag the issue from one column to another. This board here will help all of the team members by displaying the most up-to-date status.

Issues and filters

A project can have hundreds or thousands of issues and searching these issues or finding them easily could become a challenge; that's why this section in the project will help you to quickly search for the issues.

Click on **Issues and filters** | **All issues** as shown in the following screenshot:

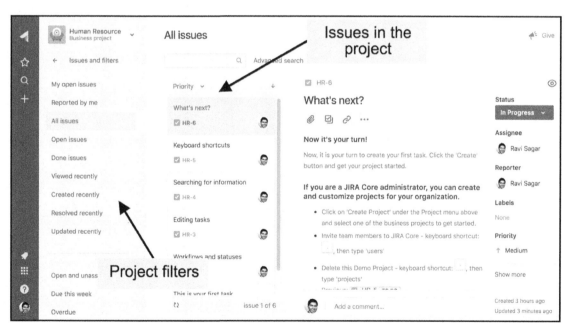

Figure 7

On the sidebar on the left-hand side, you can see all of the ready-made filters for your project such as **My open issues**, **Reported by me**, and **All issues**. Clicking on these will take you to a list of all of the issues that fulfill the criteria in that filter.

All of the issues in a specific filter are listed here; click on any of the issues and its details will open up on the right-hand side. You can do lot of things here such as change the status of the issue, add a comment, create more sub-tasks, and attach files.

There are other ways to find issues relevant to you but if you are inside a project then the scope of the issues in the **Issues and filters** section is limited to that project only.

Reports

Once you start using a project in Jira, you also want to know the progress of your work and you want to analyze the information in the project. Jira comes with ready-made reports out of the box to help you look at your data in a graphical way.

In the project sidebar, click on the reports and you'll be taken to the **All reports** section as you can see in the following screenshot:

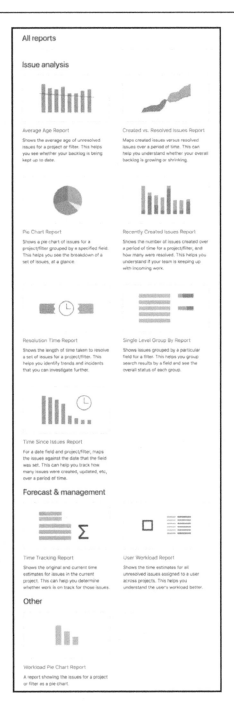

Figure 8: Jira Reports

Most of these reports are self explanatory and I highly recommend you click on any of these reports to understand what it offers; however, in Chapter 7, *Reports and Dashboards*, we'll take an in-depth look at these reports that come with a project and we'll spend time understanding how these reports can be displayed on a dashboard so that you can mix-and-match the reports that are important for you or your team on your own custom dashboard.

Working on an issue in a Jira Core project

After getting familiar with the interface of a Jira Core project, let's now create an issue in our project, understand how to work on that issue, and finally close that issue once it's complete.

Follow these steps to create a new issue and work on it:

1. Click on the **Create issue** icon on the sidebar on left-hand side as shown:

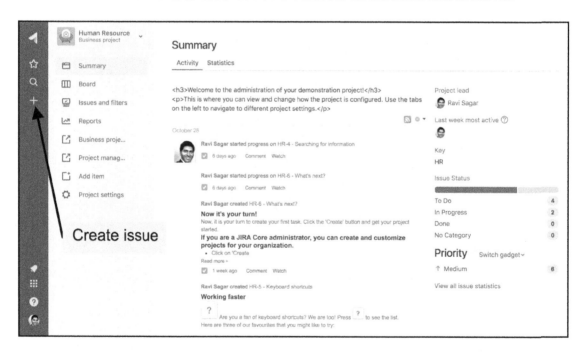

Figure 9

2. You'll be presented with a **Create issue** screen. Please fill in the relevant fields on this form such as **Issue Type** as **Task**, **Summary**, **Attachment**, **Due date**, **Description**, **Assignee**, **Priority**, **Labels**, **Original Estimate**, and **Remaining Estimate** and then click on the **Create** button. Apart from these system fields, more custom fields can also be created in Jira. The fields, their order, and whether they are mandatory or not can be customized as shown:

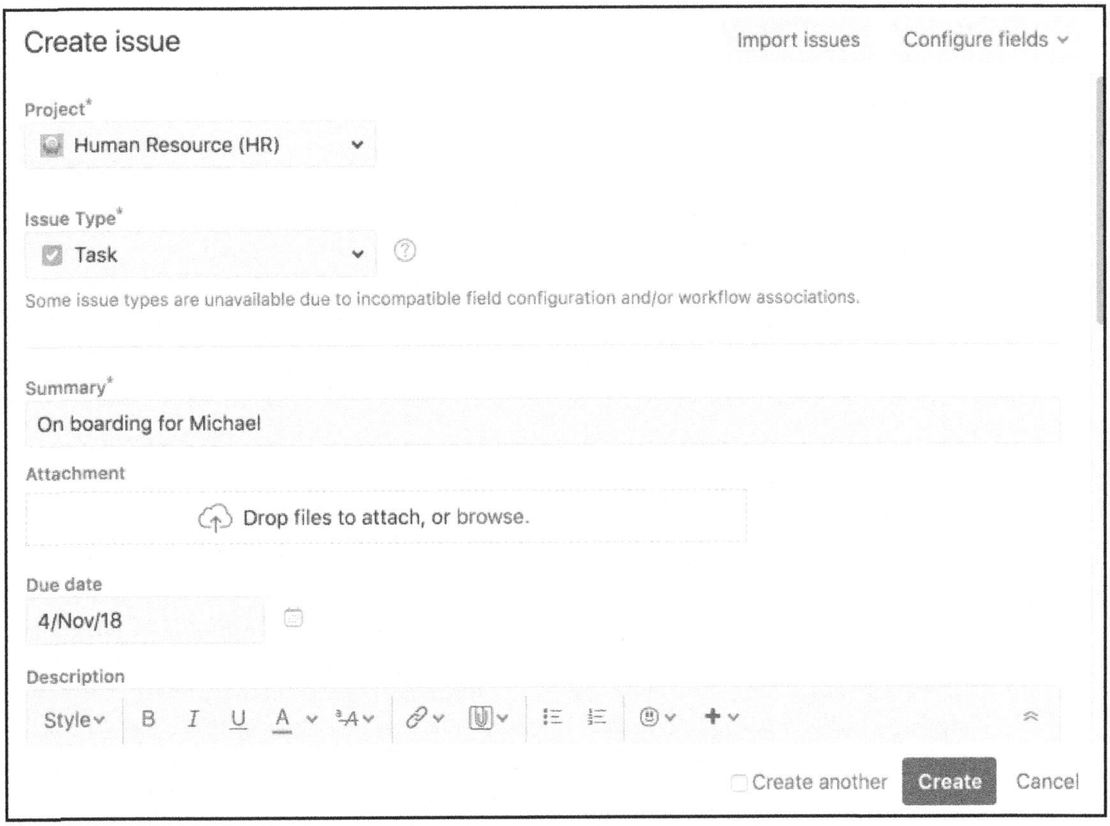

Figure 10

3. The new issue will be created and listed in both your **Summary** and **Board** sections. Click on the issue link and you'll then be taken to the **Issue View** screen, as shown in the following screenshot, where you can work on the issue:

Figure 11

4. On the **Issue View** screen, you can look at all of the available details of an issue. For instance, on top you have some buttons such as **Edit**, **Comment**, **Assign**, **Start Progress**, **Done**, and **Admin**. In the main section of the issue, you can view various fields by user such as the **Type** of an issue, which is in this case a **Task**; the **Status** of the issue; **Priority**; **Resolution**; and **Labels**. On the right side, you have information about **Assignee** and **Reporter**. This view basically displays all of the fields and lets you work on the issue.

5. Click on the **Start Progress** button on top, which is nothing but a workflow transition. The **Status** will now be changed from **TO DO** to **IN PROGRESS** as shown in the following:

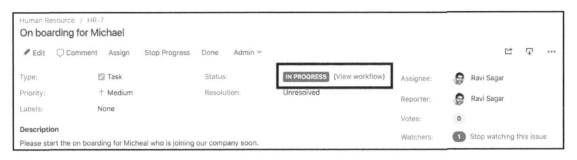

Figure 12

6. If you click on the **Done** button then the **Status** of the issues will be changed to **Done** and the **Resolution** will be changed to **Done** as well.

Congratulations, you've just learned how to work on a Jira issue from start to finish. Instead of going to the **Issue View** screen, you could also have worked on this issue from your **Board** as well by simply dragging the issue from one column to another.

Summary

In this chapter, we first asked ourselves some important questions that helped us to plan our Jira installation, then we learned how to quickly get started with using Jira Core on Cloud by first signing up for a Cloud instance and then creating a project in our application. We finally spent time understanding how to work on an issue from start to finish.

In the next chapter, we'll understand how Jira Software works; we'll first quickly go through Agile concepts and then we'll learn to create both Scrum and Kanban boards. Finally, we'll take a look at key Agile reports.

3
Using Jira Software for Development Teams

In this chapter, we'll understand how Jira Software works. We'll first learn how to enable Jira Software in our Jira Cloud instance, then we'll quickly create a new Jira Software project. We'll spend some time going through an overview of Agile concepts before looking at the Scrum and Kanban methodologies and discussing the key differences between them. Finally, we'll discuss important Jira Software reports to analyze your progress in the project.

Topics covered in this chapter include the following:

- Using Jira Software for development teams
- Overview of Agile concepts
- Is Jira suitable for development projects
- Scrum board
- Jira Software reports
- Kanban board

Using Jira Software for development teams

Jira Software is one of the most popular applications used by development teams to plan and track their projects. In the previous chapter, we discussed various aspects of Jira Core, which provides good issue tracking capabilities for business teams. Jira Software, when enabled in our instance, will provide additional features on top of what we've already seen with Jira Core.

Let's now understand how to work on Jira Software by looking at its features.

Enabling Jira Software

Jira Software, as a separate application, needs to be purchased or evaluated using a trial license and enabled in our instance.

In the rest of this book, we're going to refer to the **Site administration** section a lot to make configuration changes. You can access the **Site administration** section in the bottom-left corner of your instance, as shown in the following screenshot:

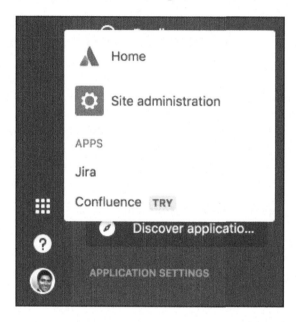

Figure 1

Perform the following steps to enable a trial subscription of Jira Software:

1. Go to **Site administration | Billing** (under **SUBSCRIPTIONS & BILLING**) | **Manage Subscriptions** and then click on **Add more Atlassian products**, as shown in the following screenshot:

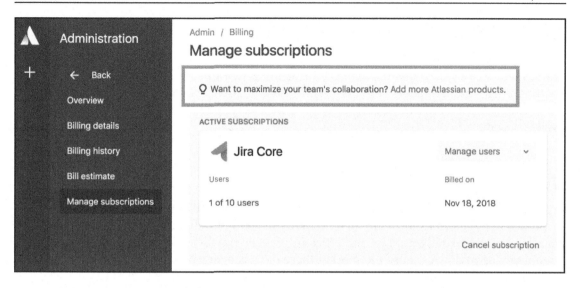

Figure 2

2. In the **Discover new products** page, click on the **Free trial** button right next to **Jira Software**, as follows:

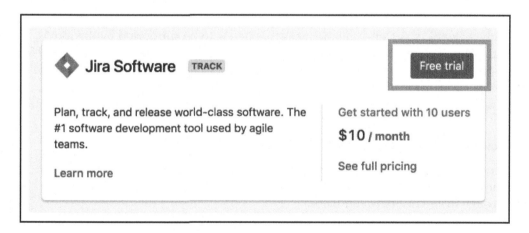

Figure 3

That's it! Your Jira Software trial is now enabled. Feel free to use it for 30 days; after that, you can always sign up for a new Jira Cloud instance or you can purchase it.

Overview of Agile concepts

We now have Jira Software enabled in our instance. It's time to create a new project and get started; however, Jira Software enables your team to work using Agile-based methodologies and supports both Scrum and Kanban; hence, before we dive straight into the features of Jira Software, it makes sense to do a very quick walk-through of various Agile concepts.

What is Agile?

Agile is just a set of values and principles for development. It's a time-boxed, iterative approach to developing software incrementally instead of delivering it all in one go, hence making it easier to deliver it fast and efficiently. Agile practices are adopted by organizations mainly because the market these days is ever evolving and the scope of the project changes during the later stages of development. The model selected for development should also incorporate changes in projects and still deliver quickly.

You can read about the 12 Agile principles by checking out the following link:

```
https://www.agilealliance.org/agile101/12-principles-behind-the-agile-manifesto/
```

One of the key objectives of Agile practices that needs to be supported by the tool is continuous improvement and continuous delivery, which are part of DevOp, a well-known buzz word these days. Jira Software can not only support Agile-based methodologies but can also provide integration with other development tools.

Scrum and Kanban methodologies

Jira Software supports both Scrum and Kanban methodologies, which are two of the most common and popular Agile-based practices. Let's understand what these are the fundamental difference between them.

Scrum is a process framework for structuring your project where work is planned first and then executed in iterations also known as Sprints. Commitment is the change agent in Scrum—that is, how much work a team can deliver is the commitment. The main idea is to deliver small usable chunks fast. After every iteration (Sprint), a working usable piece of software is expected and, as new chunks are delivered in future Sprints, they're also plugged into the existing piece of software, hence making the whole software modular. Communication within the team is key to making Scrum work for you. Scrum is more suitable for projects where planning and estimation is required, which is mostly in software projects.

Kanban focuses on incremental improvements where **Work in Progress** (**WIP**). Limit is the change agent—that is, how much work a team is currently doing is an important criteria on. As compared to Scrum, there isn't much focus on planning. A typical example of the Kanban methodology is the support desk, where work is done as it comes and, based on the number of people in the team, the amount of work a team can do needs to be visualized and improved.

We'll create projects in our Jira instance using both Scrum and Kanban to understand these fundamental differences better.

Key Agile concepts

In a moment, we'll dive into our tool again to work on an Agile-based project, but it's very important to understand some key Agile concepts or terminologies used. Some of them are explained in the following:

- **Scrum artifacts**: These include the following:
    - **Product backlog**: This is a list of tasks or issues pending in the project
    - **Sprint backlog**: A list of tasks selected for development in a specific Sprint
    - **Burndown**: This is a report that shows the progress of a Sprint
- The types of task are as follows:
    - **Epic**: This is a very high-level task that can be broken down into further tasks. Epics are similar to stories but used for better organization in the project.

- **Story**: Again, this is a high-level task that can be broken down into further tasks. Individual stories are estimated.
- **Sub-tasks**: These are the broken-down tasks of a specific story.

- **Prioritization**: This is based on rank, which is the order in which the tasks need to be completed either in a Sprint backlog or Sprint.
- **Estimation**: This is based on story points, a unit of measure for expressing the overall effort to fully implement a story. In Jira, a story point is a numeric field.
- **Iteration**: This is referred to as a Sprint. This is the actual iteration containing the list of planned estimated stories that need to be delivered within a specific period of time. Each story in a Sprint is assigned to a specific user or developer.
- **Visualization**: The following are used:
  - **Board**: A place where the status of a specific Sprint, such as how many Stories are pending, in progress, and done, can be viewed by everyone in the team.
  - Columns: A typical board has three columns—TO DO, IN PROGRESS, and DONE—showing issues based on their status, but more columns can be added if required.
  - **Swimlanes**: This is a horizontal grouping that can be created on a board to assist users when the number of stories is too many. For example, the issues on a board can be group based on the developer working on them or based on their priority.
- **Reports**: These include the following:
  - **Burndown**: One of the most popular and useful reports used to track the progress of a Sprint; on a graph, original story points are depicted versus actual story points that users are burning or completing, where the associated stories are implemented.
  - **Velocity charts**: Velocity is the average number of story points a team is delivering over a period of time. It's important to know velocity as it will help the Scrum master or project manager to plan the next Sprint more efficiently.

Roles in Agile

Now that we know various key Agile concepts, let's also go through different types of role or people involved in a typical Agile-based project, as shown in the following. We mainly need to understand what these people will be doing in our project:

- **Scrum product owner (stakeholders or business analysts)**: They define the product backlog we discussed in the previous section and write the stories need to be implemented for a successful project.
- **Scrum master (project manager or project lead)**: They'll organize Scrum meetings, define rank, estimate story points, assign work to developers, and start Sprints.
- **Scrum team (developers or testers)**: As the name suggests, these are the actual developers who will be either implementing the stories or testing them before the release.

There're certainly more roles but these three are the bare minimum you should be aware of, especially when working on a Jira project. We're now fully equipped to dive into a Jira Software project.

Is Jira suitable for development projects?

You must be wondering whether Jira Software is sufficient for your development project needs and we need to discuss some points to understand why Jira is probably the best choice for project management.

The advantages of Jira Software are as follows:

- Jira supports standard development methodologies
- It can be used out-of-the-box
- Apart from out of box templates, custom workflows can be created to support the processes
- Different roles such as developments and testers can be defined
- It supports integration with development tools such as Bitbucket, GitHub, Bamboo, and Jenkins
- Jira perfectly supports DevOps practices

Apart from using just Jira, which is a great issue-tracking tool, in Chapter 1, *Introducing Jira*, we discussed the concept of the Marketplace app to extend the features of Jira Software.

Some examples of popular apps for extending Jira features for timesheets, testing, and advanced reporting are as follows:

- Tempo Timesheet: Provide timesheet capabilities in your project
- Zephyr and X-ray: Use Jira for test management
- EazyBI: Create customized reports for your projects
- BigPicture: Create Gantt charts to plan for projects
- Portfolio: Agile road mapping and scenarios

I hope you are now eager to start using Jira straight away. So let's do that now.

Scrum board

Jira Software lets you implement the Scrum technique in your project with the help of Scrum boards. To understand the features of these tools, we'll create a project using out-of-the box templates and some sample data.

Creating a sample Scrum project

Scrum boards can be created from any existing Jira project that contains predefined issues. It's possible to create a Scrum board from a new blank project as well. Also, if you want to understand how Jira Software works, it's possible to create a sample project prepopulated with sample data.

Perform the following steps:

1. Press the / (forward slash); it'll bring up the **Search** interface on the left-hand side. Type in `boards` and click on **View all boards** (under **BOARDS**), as shown in the following screenshot:

Figure 4

2. In the **Boards** section, press the **Create board** button, as shown in the following screenshot:

Figure 5

3. In the **Create a board** popup, click on **Create a Scrum board with sample data** as shown in the following screenshot:

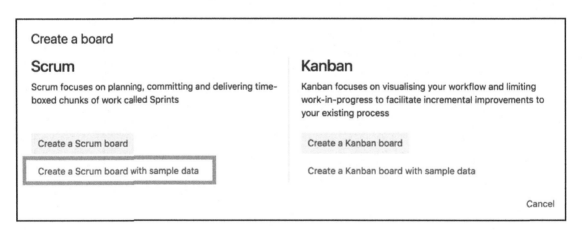

Figure 6

4. Complete the **Project name**, **Project key**, and **Project lead** fields and click on the **Create board** button, as shown in the following screenshot:

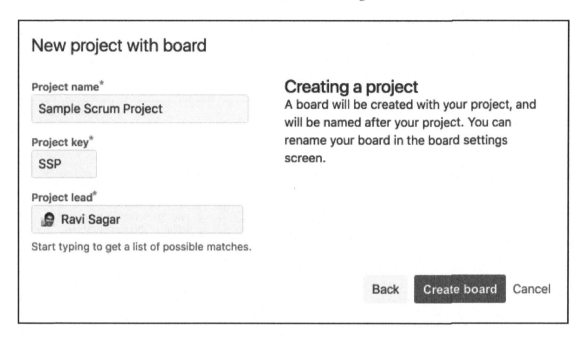

New project with board

Project name*

Sample Scrum Project

Project key*

SSP

Project lead*

Ravi Sagar

Start typing to get a list of possible matches.

Creating a project
A board will be created with your project, and will be named after your project. You can rename your board in the board settings screen.

Back   Create board   Cancel

Figure 7

We've just created a project with sample data along with a Scrum board.

Populating, ranking, and estimating a backlog using story points

In the newly created project, we have a Scrum board, which is displayed by default. You'll now see a list of issues that're pending and issues that aren't resolved yet in the **Backlog** section, and a sample Sprint, as shown in the following screenshot:

Figure 8

Backlog contains issues that're pending in the project or board. These issues are yet to be planned for execution. In the project sidebar, the first tab is **Backlog** followed by **Active sprints**. As soon as the sprint is started, you manage and work on it using the **Active sprints** tab.

The sample Scrum board already contains a Sprint that has certain issues in a specific order. A sprint is a time period during which specific planned activities need to be finished. The Scrum master or the project manager can define the order in which issues need to be completed. This order is also known as rank, and the team that's working on these issues needs to follow this order. Rank is important because there're certain tasks that need to be completed before other tasks can be started.

In a Scrum methodology, the estimation of individual tasks isn't only done on the basis of the amount of time spent, but also on the complexity of the tasks. For instance, there're two tasks with a time estimate of one day, but the first task is complex to execute because it was the first time that it was executed by the team or for some other reason. The complexity is measured by story points. The story point can be any number between 1 to 10 or any number in the Fibonacci sequence, that is, 1, 1, 2, 3, 5, 8, 13, and 21. The higher the number, the more complex the task.

The scrum master can assign story points to issues in the Sprint; although it's not mandatory to have story points with each issue in the sprint, having them will give the team an idea about the complexity of the issue.

Planning and creating sprints

The sample Scrum board already contains one running sprint; let's create a new sprint. Jira Software allows you to create another sprint even if the active sprint isn't completed, but the new sprint can't be started. However, it's possible to enable the parallel sprints feature in Jira Software that lets us run multiple sprints together.

The planning of the sprint has to be done in the Plan mode of the Scrum board. Perform the following steps to run multiple sprints together:

1. Navigate to **Jira** (under **APPS**) | **Jira Settings** | **Applications** | **Jira Software configuration** (under **JIRA SOFTWARE**), as shown here:

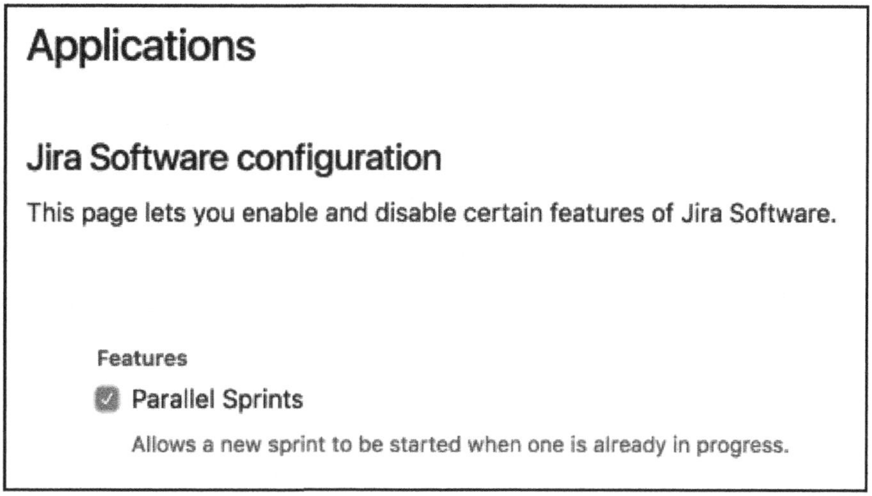

Applications

Jira Software configuration

This page lets you enable and disable certain features of Jira Software.

Features

☑ Parallel Sprints

Allows a new sprint to be started when one is already in progress.

Figure 9

2. Tick the checkbox for **Parallel Sprints**. That's it: now just go back to your board and start planning your next sprint.

3. Go back to the project and, in the **Backlog** tab, click on the **Create sprint** button just before the issue backlog, as shown in the following screenshot:

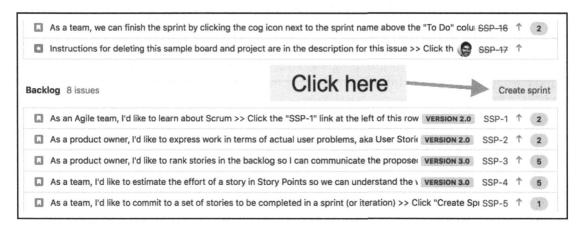

Figure 10

4. An empty sprint will be created.

5. Now, start dragging your issues from backlog to sprint, as shown here:

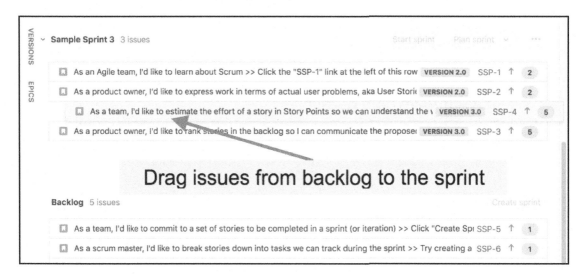

Figure 11

6. Once you've put all of your issues in the sprint, you can reorder them within the sprint and define their rank, that is, which issue needs to be performed first, second, and so on.

7. Optionally, you can also create epics to group multiple stories together. An epic is a large story and it's quite easy to create. Click on the **Create epic** link on the left-hand side of the sprint, as shown here:

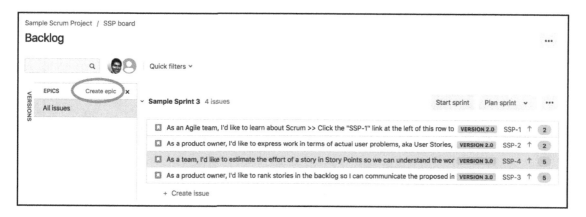

Figure 12

8. In the pop-up window, enter an **Epic Name** and **Summary**. Click on the **Create** button, as shown here, to continue:

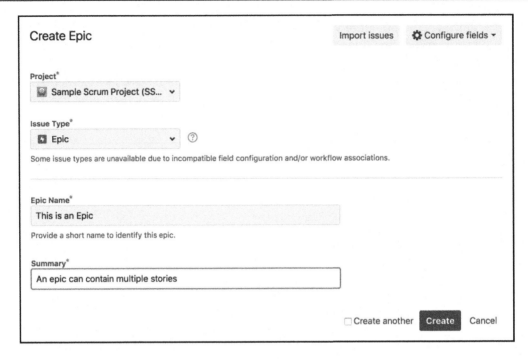

Figure 13

9. You can create more epics; finally, drag issues from your sprint to the epic. This will assign issues as part of these epics:

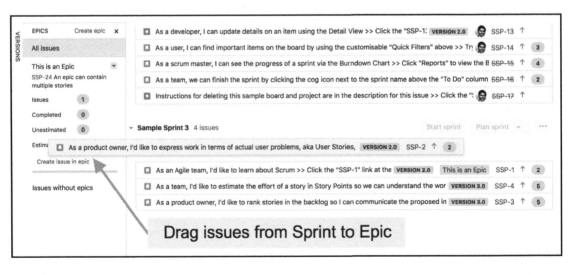

Figure 14

10. After assigning issues to the epic, you can start the sprint. Click on the **Start sprint** button at the right corner of the newly created sprint. In the pop-up window, enter a **Sprint name** and select **Duration** and **Start date** and the **End date** will be updated automatically. You can optionally also fill in the **Sprint goal**. Finally, click on the **Start** button, as shown in the following:

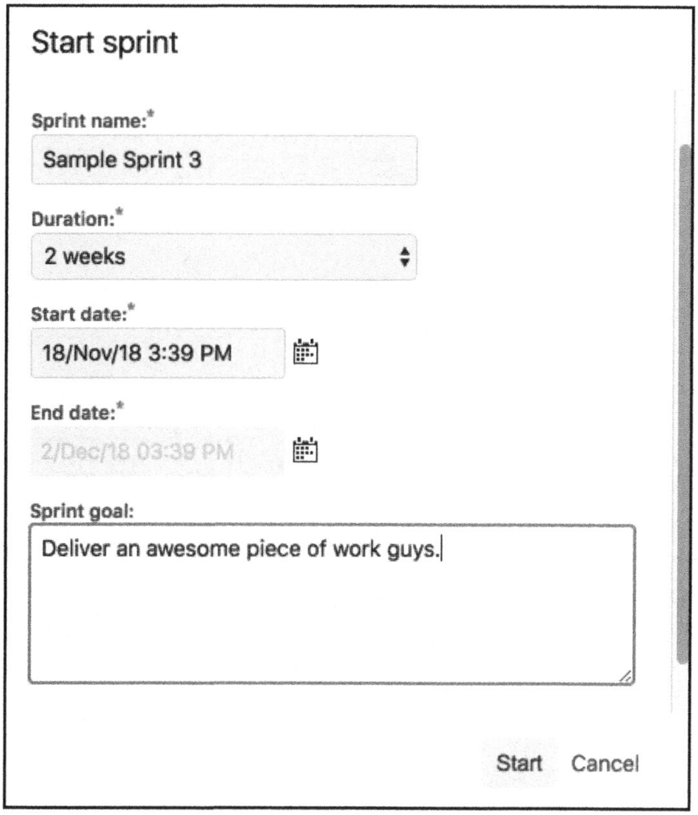

Start sprint

Sprint name:*

Sample Sprint 3

Duration:*

2 weeks

Start date:*

18/Nov/18 3:39 PM

End date:*

2/Dec/18 03:39 PM

Sprint goal:

Deliver an awesome piece of work guys.

Start   Cancel

Figure 15

Note that you should never start the sprint until you've planned your issues well, ordered them, and estimated the story points. The moment you start the sprint, you'll be taken to the **Active sprints** tab in the Scrum board. Here, you'll see a list of all of the issues in your sprints across three columns, that is, **TO DO**, **IN PROGRESS**, and **DONE**, as shown here:

Figure 16

With **Active sprints**, the individual assignee can drag the issue to any of these columns.

There are a lot of customizations that can be done in **Active sprints** to make this section more effective.

Configuring swimlanes, card colors, edit card fields, and quick filters

Active sprints is the section in the board that's monitored by team members once the sprint is running. When the number of people working on the sprint is too high, it may get difficult for them to find the issues they're working on. Let's take a look at some of the customizations done to the Scrum board. All of these options are available under the **Board settings** of a specific board, as shown here:

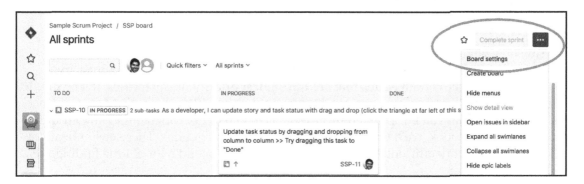

Figure 17

Click on the **Board settings** and then look at the configurations you can do in your board.

Swimlanes

The issues that appear in work mode can be grouped together so that it becomes easy for the respective member to find that issue on the board. Also, when issues are dragged from one column to another, they can only be dragged within their group, which is known as a swimlane. The default swimlane is the story issue type. The swimlane can also be based on epics and it's possible to have no swimlane at all.

Card colors

The individual issues that appear in the **Active sprints** section are displayed in a rectangular block called a card. The color of these cards can be changed based on issue types, priorities, assignees, or queries.

Card layout

The card in the **Backlog** and **Active sprints** sections displays the **Issue Id** and **Issue Summary**, but it's possible to add up to three additional fields. In total, you can add three additional fields that can appear on the card. This provision is provided so that fields that provide additional information can be made visible for the whole team to view.

Quick filters

We saw how you can customize swimlanes to group several issues. Imagine a situation when there're 20 issues in **Active sprints** that're assigned to you in the currently active sprint, but there'll be certain issues that are the highest priority. In such cases, it'll be nice to not only quickly filter out issues assigned to you, but also to filter them based on priority, such as highest. This can be achieved by adding a custom query called a JQL in your quick filter. Later in this book, we'll understand how to create JQL queries. These customizations help the team to work efficiently so that they don't need to spend a lot of time finding the relevant information.

Jira Software reports

You've learned how to plan, estimate, and start the sprint along with various configurations that we can do in the board. We checked how the team can view their tasks in the sprint. Now, it's time to monitor the progress of the team. There're two reports that're of prime importance. One is the **Burndown Chart**. This chart gives a clear picture of the current status of the sprint. The second is the **Velocity Chart**. This chart helps us understand the capacity of the team in terms of how much work it can handle. These two reports help the Scrum master monitor the progress of the project. Let's take a look at both these reports.

The Burndown Chart

While planning the sprint, we primarily did two important things. Firstly, we prioritized the order in which the issues need to be completed. Secondly, we estimated the story points for issues. These story points, which we initially planned, give an idea of the complexity of the task. Now, the moment the sprint starts, a baseline is formed between the start date and the end date. This baseline is displayed with a gray line in the chart and it depicts the ideal scenario of executing the issues from the start date of the sprint until the end date. When the issue is resolved, its story points are burned and the total remaining story points of the whole sprint decreases.

On the project slidebar, navigate to **Reports | Burndown Chart** (under Agile) and select **Sample Sprint 2**, as shown here:

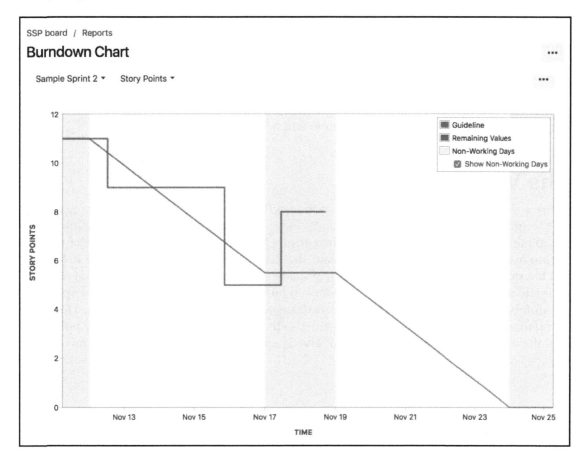

Figure 18

When the team starts working on the issues, another line—this time red—starts following the baseline. Looking at this chart, the whole team can easily figure out whether they're on or off track. If the line for **Remaining Values** is progressing above the baseline guideline, then it shows that the story points are burned slowly. Eventually, all of the issues in the sprint won't be completed.

Just after the Burndown Chart, the details of the individual issues are displayed, where you can see how many issues there were at the beginning of the sprint. As the issues are resolved, their story points are deducted from the total story points of the sprint. The total story points and the remaining story points will be displayed to the user.

The Velocity Chart

Every sprint has a total number of story points at the beginning. Ideally, the team working on the sprint should burn all of these points. In real-life cases, it's not always possible to complete all of the tasks by the end of the sprint. One of the main responsibilities of the Scrum master is to make sure that the team should have just enough story points to burn, not too many and not too few. However, at the beginning of the sprint, it's not that easy to estimate the amount of story points a team can burn. The Velocity Chart simply displays the number of story points planned versus those actually completed by the team. This comparison is shown for the past few sprints so that the average number of story points that the team can burn can be calculated. This is known as the capacity of the team.

Navigate **Reports** | **Velocity Chart** (under **Agile**) as shown here:

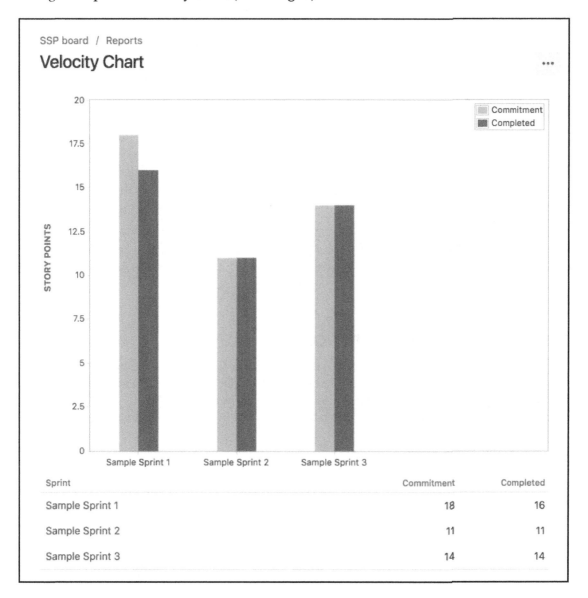

Figure 19

This chart gives us a very clear indication of the story points that the team has been able to complete in the past sprints. If you take the average of all of the story points that your team has been able to burn till now, you'll get to know your capacity. It helps the Scrum master plan the next sprint with enough resources in the team.

Kanban board

The Scrum technique is applicable in any process that requires planning, but there're various cases where the team is continuously working on activities as and when required. A typical example of this use case is customer support projects, where a certain number of people are assigned to handle the issues that're raised for a particular product or project by the company. Usually, these support issues require an immediate response and detailed planning isn't required.

In such scenarios, the overall visualization of pending issues is important. A Kanban board doesn't have any plan mode like the Scrum board. It only has work mode, which is similar to a Scrum board.

Setting up a Kanban board

A Kanban board can be created using existing projects or filters. To understand how the Kanban technique works in Jira, a sample board and project can be created just like the Scrum-based project that we created earlier. As you can notice from the following screenshot, the **Active sprints** tab isn't present in the **Kanban board**:

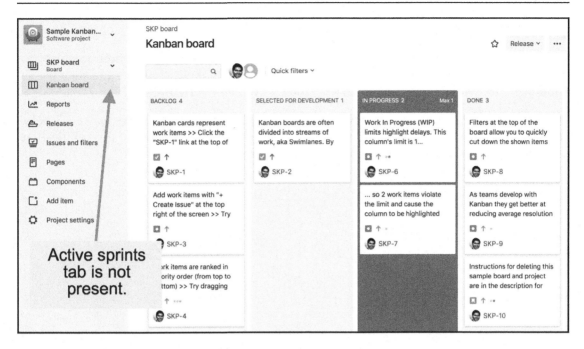

Figure 20

The team sees the **Kanban board** only. This board is quite similar to the Scrum board; you can also configure the swimlanes based on assignees; by default, the swimlanes in the Kanban board are configured to use the **priority = Highest** query. This means that issues that should be resolved immediately are displayed at the top.

The people who have these issues assigned can move the issue from one column to another. These columns signify workflow states. Most of the configurations that we did for the Scrum board can be done on the Kanban board as well.

Column constraints

When a team works on support issues, it's quite important to resolve the issues as soon as possible. Usually, companies sign SLAs—that is, Service Level Agreements—with their customers, where they need to agree on the resolution time. In situations like these, the whole team should get the overall picture of the issues that they need to work on. For instance, if there're fewer people available on support issues, then there's a limitation on the number of issues these people can work on at a given point in time. In the sample Kanban board, you can notice that the **In progress** column is red whenever there're more than one issue in it. You can change that by going to **Board settings**.

Summary

In this chapter, you learned how to implement Scrum and Kanban Agile methodologies using Jira Software. We first spent some time understanding Agile concepts and then we understood how to use both boards in Jira along with their configurations.

In the next chapter, we'll discuss how to implement Jira Service Desk to take care of IT help desks and support desks. We'll see the various features and functionality of this application and how you can customize them to make it work for you as well.

4
Using Jira Service Desk for Help Desks

In this chapter, we'll discuss how to implement a help desk using Jira Service Desk to take care of IT help desk and support requests, which isn't just easy to use but also comes with pre-configured features of a ticketing system out of the box.

We'll first begin with various aspects of a typical help desk system, then we'll quickly create a Jira Service Desk project and go through its various features to understand how it can help us implement a great service desk.

Topics covered in this chapter include the following:

- Using Jira Service Desk for help desks
- Overview of help desks
- Creating a Jira Service Desk project
- Configure Jira Service Desk
- Jira Service Desk reports

Using Jira Service Desk for help desks

Jira Service Desk is the fastest growing Atlassian product because it makes it so easy for a help desk team to manage its work. So far in this book, we've been discussing various aspects of Jira. We've already covered Jira Core and Jira Software features by creating projects to understand how you and your team can use this intuitive tool to manage tasks and development activities. Jira Service Desk was built while keeping in mind customer satisfaction first and foremost, and making it very simple for any customer to raise and track their tickets in Jira Service Desk using a friendly customer portal; at the same time, technicians (also known as agents) work on those tickets using a familiar Jira interface.

Enabling Jira Service Desk

In Chapter 3, *Using Jira Software for Development Teams*, we learned how to enable new applications by going to the **Manage Subscription** section under **Billing**. Please do the same thing and enable Jira Service Desk on your cloud instance.

After enabling Jira Service Desk, you'll have 30 days to evaluate or learn it.

Overview of Helpdesk

So, now you're anxious to create a project in Jira Service Desk but it makes more sense to first go through the basics of a typical help desk system and understand its various aspects. These concepts will help you understand Jira Service Desk better.

Basic features of any help desk

Let's do a quick walk-through of various aspects and features of a typical help desk:

- **Different user roles—customers and agents:** In a help desk, there're primarily two types of users; one is your customer, who will raise a ticket on the system to get help from the service or support desk. The agent, on the other hand, will respond to the tickets and provide help to the customers.
- **Service level agreement:** Customers expect a quick resolution of their tickets. You can't expect them to wait indefinitely after raising a ticket. The service level agreement, also commonly known as SLA, defines how quickly agents will respond and resolve the ticket. Multiple SLAs can be defined and agreed with the customer or your client when providing services to them. SLAs are nothing but a time frame within which agents will do a certain action such as resolving tickets.
- **Email notifications:** Any help desk tool provides a platform for both customers and agents to interact with each other; however, sending email alerts to your customers will ensure that a ticket has been successfully raised and received by the support team. During the lifecycle of the ticket, on many occasions an email notification can be sent to involved parties; this is to ensure that the appropriate action is taken on time.

- **Ability to engage with customers:** The ticket, when raised by the customer, can be resolved directly by an agent or further information is needed by an agent to take further action on the ticket. Agents can also interact with the customer by posting comments on the ticket for customers and they can also reply by typing comments. It's a great way to have interaction between them.
- **Reports:** The service desk team manager wants to take a look at various analytics to understand how well his or her team is performing. There're many questions that manager will ask, such as: How many ticket did we resolve last month? How many times was the SLA breached? Are we overbooked? How many tickets are currently open? Answers to these questions can be found by looking at reports in a service desk tool.

Let's now look at common help desk processes.

Help desk processes

Help desks can be used to provide support to customers by handling their tickets. The tickets can be of different types and the way agents work on the tickets can be different based on the nature of the request. The way a ticket is handled is defined by the process behind it. Processes define how to handle different types of requests

The most common help desk processes are as follows:

- **Incident management**: *Website is down* is an incident
- **Problem management**: *Website is down almost every week* could be due to a problem
- **Change management**: *Update the database version* is a change
- **Service request**: *Please reset my password* is a service request

There're many other processes, such as release management and knowledge management; if you want to know more about them, please read about ITIL (formerly an acronym for Information Technology Infrastructure Library), which is a set of detailed practices for **IT Service Management (ITSM)**.

Now we have the necessary background to start working on Jira Service Desk.

Different ways to raise tickets

Tickets are usually raised by customers and handled by agents; however, you must be wondering: How will a customer raise a ticket?

In Jira, there're four different ways to raise tickets in Jira Service Desk:

- **Customer portal**: This is a web-based interface integrated with the knowledge base in Confluence
- **Email**: A customer can send an email to the help desk
- **Jira Service Desk**: An agent can raise a ticket on behalf of a customer
- **RESTful API**: A ticket can be raised programmatically

It's important to know about them because, in Jira Service Desk, these different ways to raise tickets are known as channels. For the help desk or service desk manager, it's very important to know the number of tickets raised through a specific channel.

Creating a Jira Service Desk project

Let's create a Jira Service Desk project in our instance. We've already enabled a Jira Service Desk subscription in our instance.

Perform the following steps to create a Jira Service Desk project:

1. Go to **Jira settings** | **Projects** and then click on the **Create project** button in the top-right corner, as shown here:

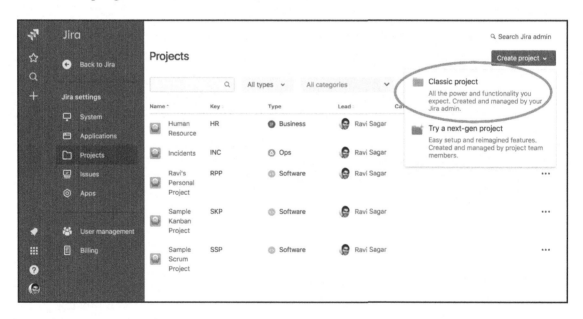

Figure 1

2. Click on **Classic project | Change template** and select **IT service desk**, as shown here:

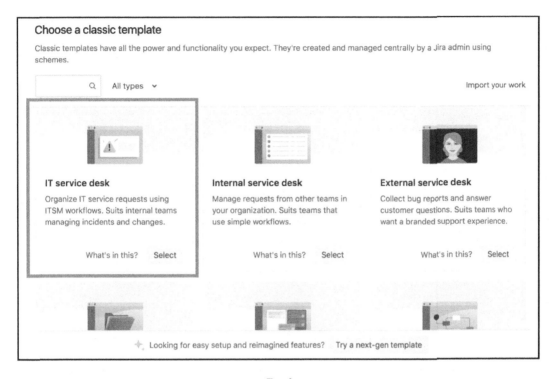

Figure 2

3. In the **Create project** screen, enter the **Name** of the project and click on the **Create** button, as shown here:

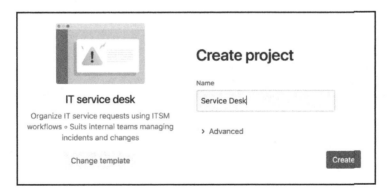

Figure 3

4. Your new Jira Service Desk project is ready. The screen will be similar to the following:

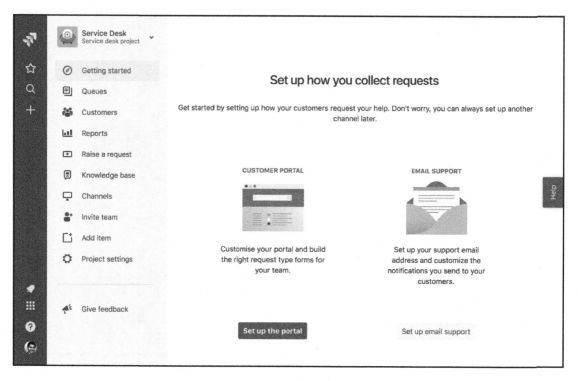

Figure 4

You can start using this project straightaway as the IT service desk template comes with out-of-the-box configurations; however, we'll go through various aspects of the project to understand how you can customize it to make it more aligned to your specific requirements.

Using Jira Service Desk

Congratulations on creating your first Jira Service Desk project! Although you can start using it out-of-the-box, we want to learn important aspects of it, starting with the customer portal, which is the web interface customers can use to raise tickets and reach out to you.

Customer portal

The most important purpose of the Service Desk application is to focus on a support request and ticketing system to cater to the requests of end users and customers. Using Jira, a simple project can be created to track issues and access can be given to customers, provided there're enough licenses; however, but in general, end users may not find it intuitive to log in to an issue tracker to raise their requests. Atlassian understood this concern and created a Service Desk application with a dedicated customer portal, which is a quite neat and simple interface on which to raise support requests.

Every Service Desk project will have its own customer portal URL like the following:

```
https://JIRAURL/servicedesk/customer/portal/1
```

You'll find this URL when you click on the **Raise a request** tab in the project sidebar. You can share this URL with your customers or publish it on your website. The customer portal offers a simple and intuitive interface to raise the request. Let's go through this portal; please open this URL in your web browser. You'll see a screen similar to the following:

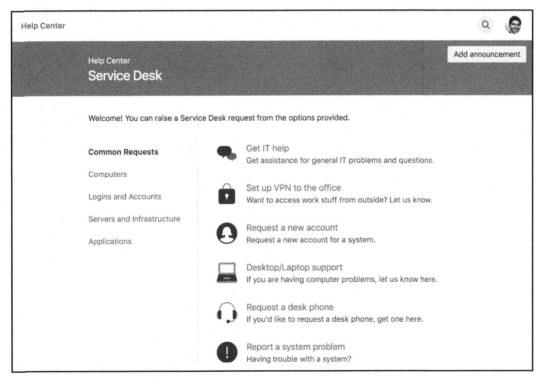

Figure 5

On the left side, various groups are listed and, under each of them, several requests types, such as **Get IT help**, **Set up VPN to the office**, and **Request a new account**, are listed. These request types are actually assigned to a specific issue type in Jira. We can create a new request type and map it to any existing issue type.

Click on **Report a system problem** to open a new page with a form to raise a request, as shown here:

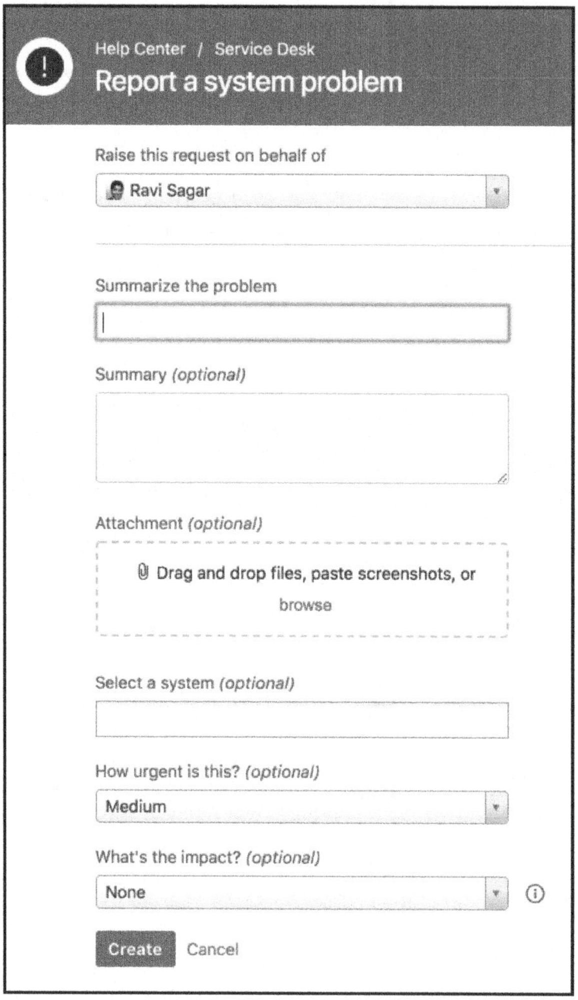

Figure 6

Customers can fill in this form and click on the **Create** button to raise the request.

Once the request is submitted, a Jira issue is created for the service desk agent in the project.

The customer portal can be further customized; please refer to the following links to find out more:

- **Customizing the help center**: `https://confluence.atlassian.com/servicedeskcloud/customize-the-help-center-954239157.html`
- **Configuring the portal**: `https://confluence.atlassian.com/servicedeskcloud/configuring-the-customer-portal-732528918.html`

Queues

A queue is simply a filtered list of issues based on predefined conditions. For instance, there're several queues already defined in your project such as **All open**, **Assigned to me**, **Unassigned issues**, **Incidents**, **Service requests**, **Change**, and **Problem**. You can find them when you click on **Queues** in your project sidebar.

You can also create your own queues. Go to **Queues** and click on the **New queue** link, the result is shown in the following screenshot:

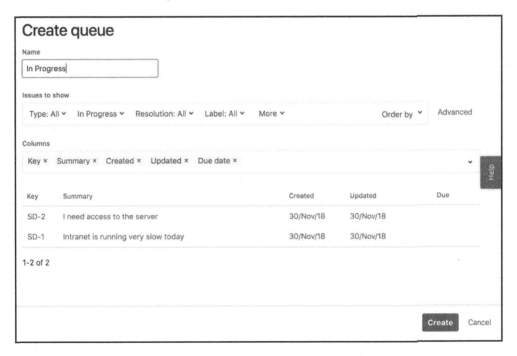

Figure 7

In the **Create queue** screen, under **Name** enter In Progress and, under **Issues to show**, select **Status** as **In Progress**. If you're familiar with JQL, then click on the **Advanced** link right next to the **Issues to show** section. Press the **Create** button to save the queue.

The queue will now be saved and available in the existing list of queues in your project.

Customer permissions

Your Service Desk project is by default open for everyone to raise tickets but we can limit which user or group is a customer and can raise requests in this project.

Go to **Customer | Change permissions** to manage who can raise tickets, as shown in the following:

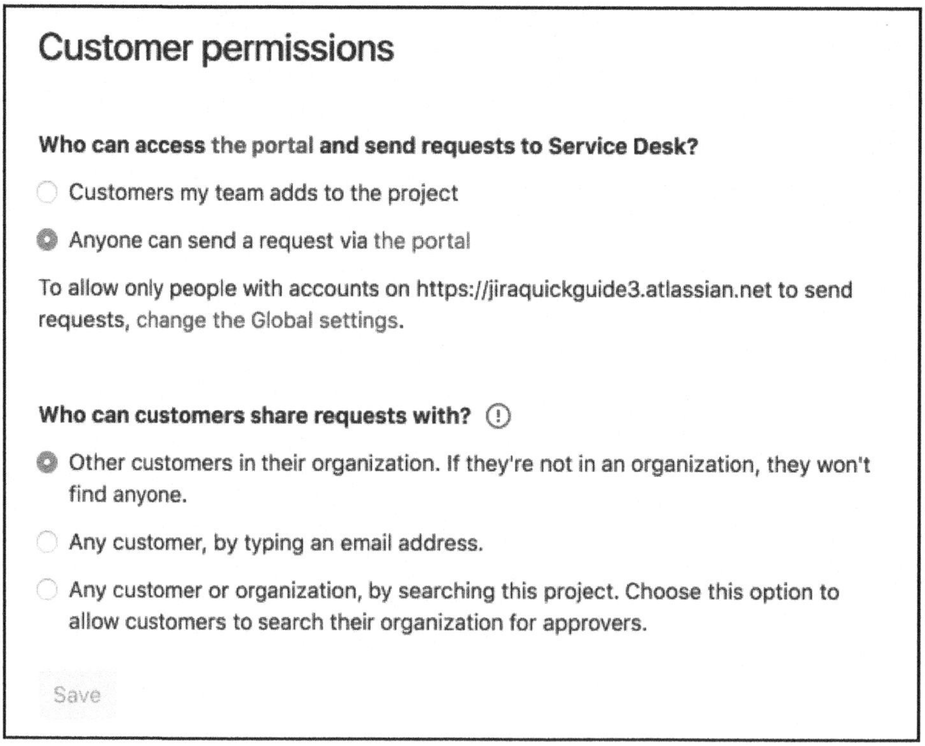

Customer permissions

Who can access the portal and send requests to Service Desk?

○ Customers my team adds to the project

⦿ Anyone can send a request via the portal

To allow only people with accounts on https://jiraquickguide3.atlassian.net to send requests, change the Global settings.

Who can customers share requests with? ⓘ

⦿ Other customers in their organization. If they're not in an organization, they won't find anyone.

○ Any customer, by typing an email address.

○ Any customer or organization, by searching this project. Choose this option to allow customers to search their organization for approvers.

Save

Figure 8

Here you can also opt to let customers further share tickets from the customer portal with other customers.

Configuring Jira Service Desk

There're various configurations available in Jira Service Desk. These options are available under the **Project settings** of your project. The majority of these configurations are specific to a Jira Service Desk project and define how your customers will interact with the Service Desk.

Let's look at the important configurations.

Request types

Earlier, we discussed the customer portal, which is a simple interface for end users. They get to choose the different types of request, which are internally mapped to a specific **Issue type**. Under this section, you can create a new request type and modify existing ones, as shown in the following:

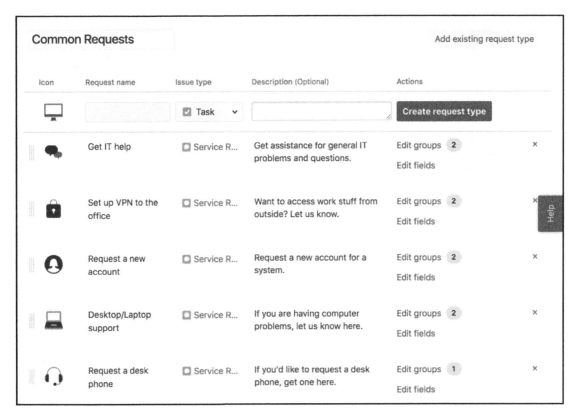

Figure 9

Enter the **Request name**, such as **Hardware problem**, select **Issue type** as **Problem**, enter **Description**, and press the **Create request type** button. Now, if you go back to your customer portal, there'll be a new request type added, but it'll only contain the **Summary** field. Let's now add a few more fields to this request type, as shown in the following:

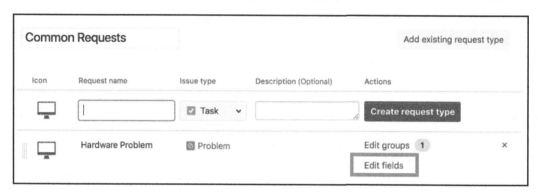

Figure 10

Click on the **Edit fields** link corresponding to the request type you want to modify, as shown:

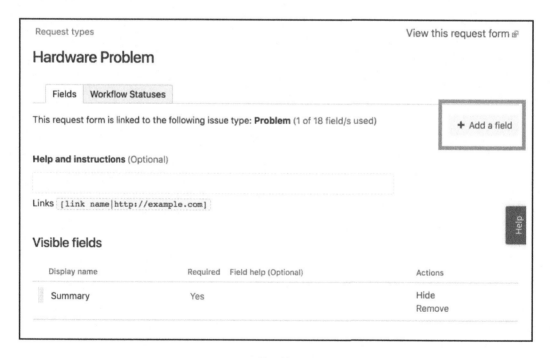

Figure 11

Now click on the **Add a field** button on the top-right corner of the screen; the result is shown in the following:

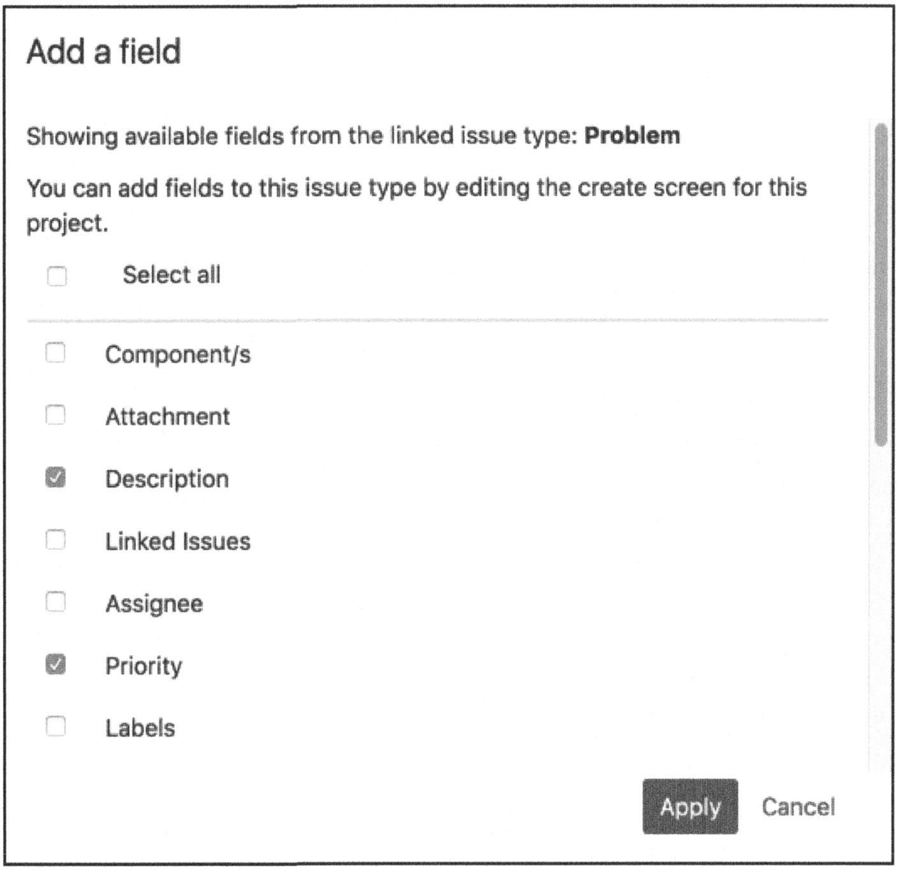

Add a field

Showing available fields from the linked issue type: **Problem**

You can add fields to this issue type by editing the create screen for this project.

☐   Select all

☐   Component/s

☐   Attachment

☑   Description

☐   Linked Issues

☐   Assignee

☑   Priority

☐   Labels

                          Apply   Cancel

Figure 12

In the **Add a field** popup, select the fields that you want to add and press the **Apply** button.

The fields will now be added and will be visible to the end user on the customer portal. You can also make some fields as required under this section.

Portal settings

In this section, you can change the **Name** of your customer portal, which is by default the same as your project name, and you can upload a custom logo.

It's also possible to give an announcement to the users that will be displayed on top of your customer portal.

Email requests

Apart from the customer portal, you can configure Jira Service Desk in such a way that your customers can raise tickets by simply sending an email to a specific email address. We need to configure our project first to enable this functionality.

Click on the **Turn on email requests** button as shown in the following:

Figure 13

On the next screen, click on the **Add a custom email address** button; the result is shown in the following:

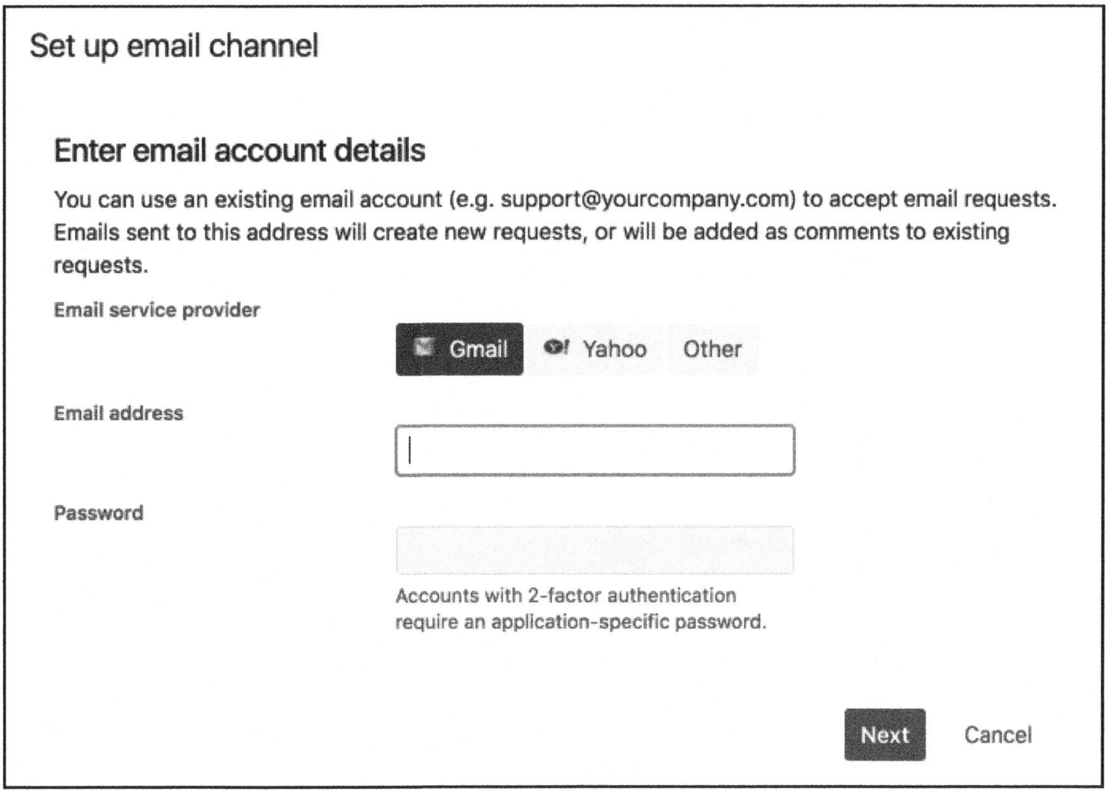

Set up email channel

Enter email account details

You can use an existing email account (e.g. support@yourcompany.com) to accept email requests. Emails sent to this address will create new requests, or will be added as comments to existing requests.

Email service provider

      Gmail   Yahoo   Other

Email address

Password

Accounts with 2-factor authentication require an application-specific password.

Next   Cancel

Figure 14

In the **Set up email channel** popup, enter the details of your email account. If you're using a Google Apps account, then enter the **Email address** and **Password**, but you can also configure POP- and IMAP-based accounts from the **Other** tab. Press the **Next** button to continue. The following screen will be displayed:

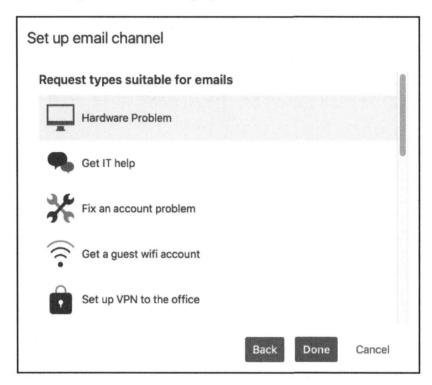

Figure 15

Now you'll need to select which request type will be used to create issues from email and press the **Done** button at the bottom.

The email will now be configured with this project. Jira Service Desk will continuously read the specified inbox and, whenever there's a new mail, it'll copy the email subject in the **Summary** field and the email content in the **Description** field.

Satisfaction settings

In the Service Desk project, your customers can give feedback. This will help you understand how satisfied they are. Under this section, you can enable or disable this feature.

Knowledge base

Service Desk projects can be integrated with a Confluence space. This is useful: when customers raise a request through the customer portal, they can be presented with the related pages on Confluence. Customers can then go through those related pages and can possibly solve their problems and may not need to raise a request. The integration with Confluence can be done under this section, where you can specify which space in your Confluence will be linked to your Jira Service Desk project.

SLAs

Service Desk projects come with some pre-configured service level agreements, also known as SLAs. Some common SLAs are listed as follows:

- **Time to resolution**: Time taken from creation to resolution of the issue
- **Time to first response**: Time taken from creation to a comment being added for a customer

We can also create our own SLA, such as **Time to assign**. Perform the following steps to create a new SLA in your project:

1. Click on the **New Metric** link on the left side
2. In the **New Metric** screen, enter the **Name:** of the metric as `Time to assign`
3. Select the **Start** time when the count will begin
4. Select the **Stop** time when the count will finish
5. Under the **Goals** section, enter the **Goal** as **4h** for **All remaining issues** and press the **Update** button

6. Press the **Create** button on top to save the new SLA, as shown in the following:

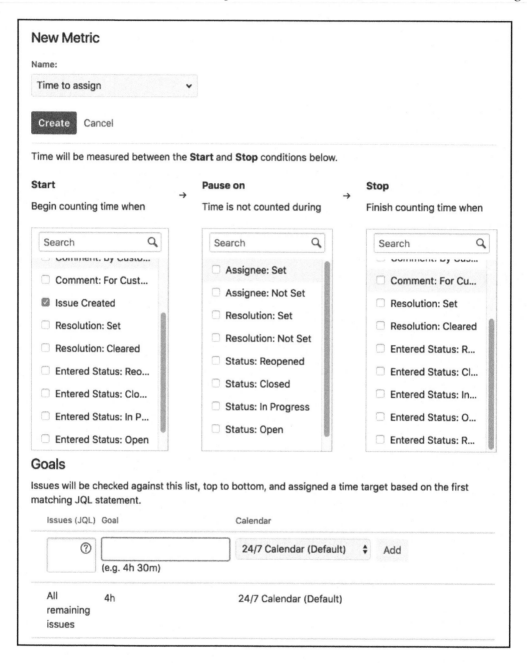

Figure 16

The new SLA will be reflected in all existing and new issues in your project. In this section, you can also configure calendars with working days, working time, and holidays. The SLA clock will stop outside working hours and these calendars can be mapped to any SLAs. The SLA goal that we defined could be for all issues in the project or for a subset of issues based on the JQL in the SLA configurations.

Automation

Service Desk projects come with a nifty utility you can use to add some automation tasks in the project. This utility assists the team with performing recurring tasks and enforcing some policies.

For instance, we just added a new SLA time to assign the issue to an agent within four hours of its creation. We could actually post a comment on the request when only 60 minutes are remaining in this SLA. This comment would be visible only to existing agents assigned to this project.

To add a new rule, click in the **Add rule** button on the top-right corner, as shown in the following:

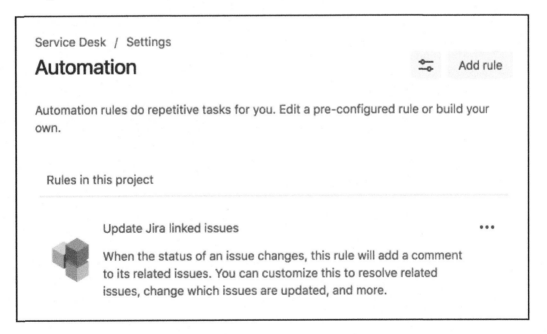

Figure 17

In the **New automation rule** popup, select **Create a custom rule** and press the **Continue** button:

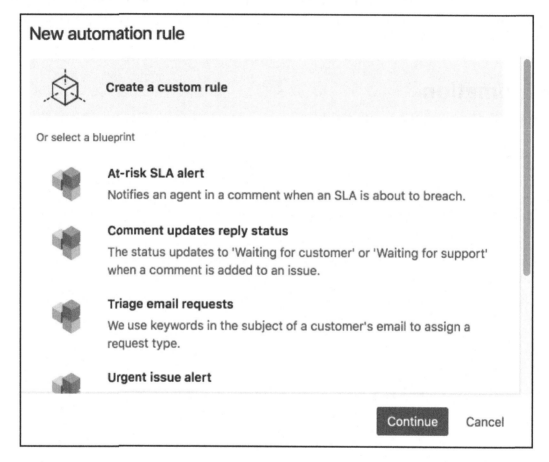

Figure 18

In the next screen, we now have to **Add trigger** under **When this happens** and we have to **Add action** under **Then do this**:

Figure 19

Click on the **Add trigger,** select **SLA time remaining** as **Time to assign** and press the **Add** button. Just make sure **Event** is set to **Due soon (60 min remaining),** as shown:

Figure 20

Now click on **Add action**, select **Add comment**, select **Comment type** as **Internal**, and press the **Add** button as shown in the following:

Figure 21

We've now added a new rule that will post an internal comment on the issue when the SLA is due in the next 60 minutes; based on your notification schemes in the project, you might also receive an email notification from Jira Service Desk.

Jira Service Desk reports

The Service Desk project comes with some really good built-in reports that'll help you understand the current progress of your team working on the support project.

Let's understand the purpose of these reports. These reports are available under your project sidebar if you click on the **Reports** link.

Workload

This is a simple report that shows the number of requests your team is working on right now. It'll help you to evenly distribute the workload among your agents. The reports displays the number of issues in progress for each agent. This is an important report that helps the project lead evenly distribute the work among agents so they aren't under-or-over allocated.

SLA goals

Service Desk comes with an SLA such as time to first response and time to resolution. This report will tell you whether your team is able to achieve these SLA goals or not. The report displays the percentage of successful achievement for the SLA in the last seven days. These reports can quickly tell you how the team's performing in resolving issues measured by time-bound goals.

Satisfaction

This report will display the average customer satisfaction. This usually helps you understand whether your customers are happy with your service or not. It displays an average of ratings given by the users. It's a nice and quick way to get general feedback from users and can help you understand their satisfaction level.

Requests deflected

If you've linked a Confluence space with your project, then this report shows the number of times articles were viewed and how many customers found those articles useful, and hence didn't raise any tickets and were able to serve themselves. Jira Service Desk is closely integrated with the Confluence space by providing related articles to the user while they're raising a new request, which might be a known issue or a very common request. In such cases, an article in the linked Confluence space can help users to serve themselves.

Requests resolved

This reports shows the number of requests resolved with an article, requests resolved without an article, and requests deflected in the portal. The statistics shown here will help you to understand the effectiveness of your knowledge base.

Created versus resolved

This reports displays the number of issues created versus resolved for the selected duration such as the past seven days, the past 14 days, or the past 30 days. A similar report is usually present in non-Jira Service Desk projects too.

Time to resolution

This report shows how much time is taken to resolve all of the issues, along with how much time is taken to resolve issues of a particular type, such as incidents.

SLA met versus breached

This is a simple count of how many issues achieved their SLA goal versus how many issues didn't achieve their SLA goals or, in other words, were breached.

Incidents reported by priority

A count of issues based on individual priorities is displayed in this report. It's useful to get a quick glimpse of the issue count broken up by priorities such as highest, high, medium, low, and lowest.

There're other similar reports available in a Jira Service Desk project that you can also customize further; you can also create your own.

Summary

In this chapter, you learned how to use Jira Service Desk in your instance and understood the various configuration options it has to offer to make projects more relevant to your business needs.

Now you have enough knowledge of Jira fundamentals and you know how Jira Core, Jira Software, and Jira Desk Service projects are different from each other and their unique offerings. In the next chapter, we'll start with customizing Jira, which is applicable to all three types of Jira applications. We'll first start with understanding the concept of Jira Schemes and then we'll learn how to customize a workflow in our project.

Jira Schemes and Configuring Project Workflow

5

In this chapter, we will begin customizing Jira. Thus far, we have covered the basic functionality of the tool and have gone through the unique features of Jira Core, Jira Software, and Jira Service Desk. Learning how to customize Jira will help you tweak it for your own specific requirements.

We will begin with understanding the concept of Jira schemes and then we will learn how to customize a workflow in our project.

Topics covered in this chapter include the following:

- The various types of user in Jira
- An overview of various schemes in Jira
- Customizing Jira workflow

The various types of user in Jira

At the beginning of the book, we created a new Jira instance, where we created new projects and also worked on those projects to understand the features. We were able to do that only because we also have the full admin rights on our instance. In Jira, however, not everyone can be an administrator.

Primarily, there are three types of users in Jira, and these are as follows:

- User
- Project administrator
- Jira administrator

User

Anyone who can log in to Jira is a user and, in most cases, a user will consume a Jira license as well, except in Jira Service Desk, where customers don't count toward the license.

A user is typically your developers or testers in the development team, and an agent in the service desk team. In most cases, users will work on their issues and tasks. More permissions can, however, be assigned to a user.

Project administrator

Project administrators are usually managers or leads. They are responsible for the whole project. They are quite similar to users, but usually have more rights in relation to the project. For instance, they can add people to a project, manage project milestones, and they have more authority as regards actual issues.

Jira administrator

Apart from users and project administrators, Jira administrators have the authority to manage your Jira instance. They can create projects, users, customize project workflows, add more custom fields, and are also responsible for the performance of the whole instance.

Jira administrators usually receive requests from other people to customize their projects. Ideally, you should not give this permission to many people in your team. Only a few people should have responsibility for managing your instance.

Overview of various schemes in Jira

When you create a project in Jira, the first thing that you do is create some issues under it. When the issues are created, you may want to assign it to someone. The person who is supposed to work on the issue will then start working on the issue and will eventually resolve it. It is a very simple example of the life cycle of the issue in Jira, but there are many things happening in the background.

The way you work on the project, the kinds of issue you create, the fields you capture in the issue, and its life cycle stages and behavior, are defined by various schemes in a Jira project.

The project that we created earlier in this book involved utilizing the default template that comes with Jira. The default templates are nothing but a collection or set of various schemes. These templates help us to get started with Jira very quickly and, based on your development methodology, you can choose from various types of templates that are based on standard practices observed in the industry.

However, every team is different, and they may have their own expectations from a Jira project. Further customization can be done either on a project-by-project basis, or according to a set of projects using the same set of schemes, prior to modifying them. Let's quickly understand the purpose of the various schemes in Jira.

Issue type schemes

In Jira, we can have different issue types, such as Epic, Story, Task, and Bug. You can always create more issue types if you want. Issue type schemes define which issue types will be available within a particular project.

A typical scrum-based project in Jira software would have Story, Bug, Epic, Task, and Sub-task, which is defined by the issue type scheme used in the project. One scheme can always be shared by other projects in Jira.

Workflow schemes

Workflow defines the life cycle of an issue in Jira. Within a project, you can have one workflow for all the issue types or separate workflows for each one of them. If you are using Jira Core with issue types such as Task and Sub-task, then creating a single workflow with three statuses: Open, In Progress and Closed—would work, but, for a software development project, you may want to have separate workflows for Bug and Story.

Workflow schemes define which workflow will be used by which issue type in the project. The following table provides you with some examples of workflow schemes:

Project	Issue types	Workflows
Legal project	Task Contract	Legal workflow (Task and Contract)
Software project	Epic Story Bug Task	Agile Workflow (Epic and Story) Defect Workflow (Bug and Task)

When new workflows are created, you can attach them to an existing issue type in the same workflow scheme used in the project. For example, in our preceding software project, if, in future, a third workflow is needed for Epic, it can be done by simply modifying an existing workflow scheme.

Issue type screen schemes

When you create issues in Jira, the pop-up window where you fill in the details is nothing but a screen. It is a collection of fields. You would normally use screens to add/remove fields.

In Jira, screens are associated with three operations: create, edit, and view.

Different screens can be used when you create an issue, when you edit it, and when you are looking at the issue.

A screen scheme defines the mapping of the screen and an operation.

The issue type screen scheme defines the mapping of the screen scheme and an issue type.

Field configuration schemes

When you create an issue in your project, you may have already noticed that some fields are mandatory, especially project, issue type, and summary, but if you want to make other fields mandatory as well, then you need to do that using field configurations. The other purpose of field configurations is to also hide certain fields completely.

The behavior of the field that you define—Required/Hidden is also mapped to the issue type. For instance, a field such as Due Date can be made mandatory for Bug, but not an Epic in the same project.

Permission schemes

Once you have access to the project, then everything that you can do within that project is defined by the permission scheme configured for that project. There are various permissions related to who creates issues, edits issues, closes issues, adds a comment, adds attachments, and much more.

When a new project is created, it comes with a default permission scheme that can be modified further if required. The individual permissions within a scheme can be given to an individual, project role, or a group of users in Jira.

Notification schemes

Jira can send email alerts to various people regarding different events. When the new issue is created, an email can be sent to the reporter of the issues. There are various events related to the issue and the workflow transitions. These notifications are configured for a variety of such events and can be modified if you don't want to receive lots of emails from the system.

Now that we know the purpose of various schemes, let's now modify the software project that we created earlier and create a new workflow.

Customizing Jira workflow

In `Chapter 3`, *Using Jira Software for Development Teams*, we created a Jira software project and familiarized ourselves with its various functionalities. We created a sample scrum project that comes with predefined configurations and schemes for scrum-based methodologies.

Open **Sample Scrum Project** and go to **Project settings | Workflows.**

You will notice that there is a workflow scheme with one workflow already in that project used by all the available issue types. In the following screen, if you click on the **diagram** link, you will then be able to look at the workflow associated with the project:

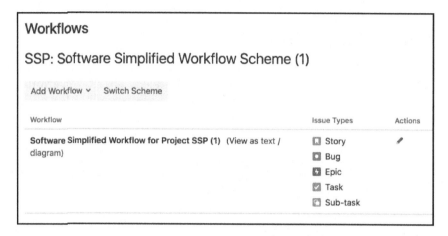

Figure 1

As you can see on the following screen, the workflow has three states: **TO DO, DONE,** and **IN PROGRESS**. The **All** sign signifies that you can go to any state directly; in other words, you don't have to follow a specific path in order to resolve the issue:

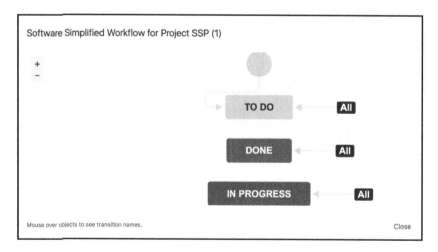

Figure 2

The preceding workflow is already working well, but we want to create our own workflow, similar to this one, but with a few specific requirements, as mentioned in the following:

- Add a new state: **ON HOLD**.
- The issue cannot be sent to **DONE** directly. It has to go through the **IN PROGRESS** status first.

The following diagram represents the workflow that we will be creating and using in our project for the Bug issue type only:

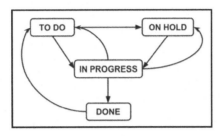

Figure 3

New status

In the proposed new workflow, there is a new status called **ON HOLD**, which we first need to create in our Jira instance.

Go to **Jira settings** | **Issues** | **Statuses** (under **ISSUE ATTRIBUTES**) and click on the **Add status** button in the top-right corner.

Enter `On Hold` under **Name,** and `Issue is on hold` under **Description,** and then click on the **Add** button to create a new status, demonstrated as follows:

Figure 4

Creating a new workflow

Let's now create our new workflow.

Go to **Jira settings** | **Issues** | **Workflows** (Under **WORKFLOWS**) and click on the **Add workflow** button in the top-right corner and enter the **Name** as `Bug workflow`, `This is the Bug workflow` under **Description,** and then click on the **Add** button, as demonstrated in the following screenshot:

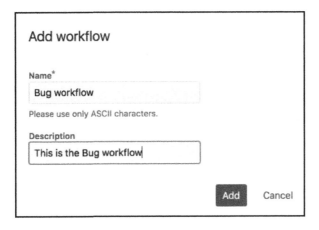

Figure 5

On the next screen, you will be presented with the options to edit the workflow. There are two modes to edit the workflow—**Diagram** and **Text**, both the modes will more or less let you do the same thing with few options available to each mode but we will be using the Diagram mode to create our workflow.

Click on the **Add status** option on the left-hand side and add the **TO DO, IN PROGRESS, ON HOLD,** and **DONE** statuses in your workflow, demonstrated as follows:

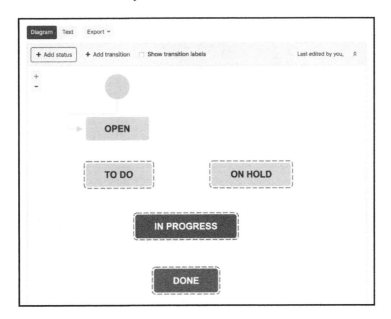

Figure 6

The statues will now be added to your workflow. We have made some progress, but we still need to do a few more things, primarily, removing unwanted statuses, adding transitions, and changing the Create transition to start from **TO DO** instead of **OPEN** state, this will ensure that the first state in the workflow is **TO DO.**

Click on **Create transition** and change it to begin with from the **OPEN** status to the **TO DO** status instead by simply dragging the arrow and dropping it on **TO DO,** demonstrated as follows:

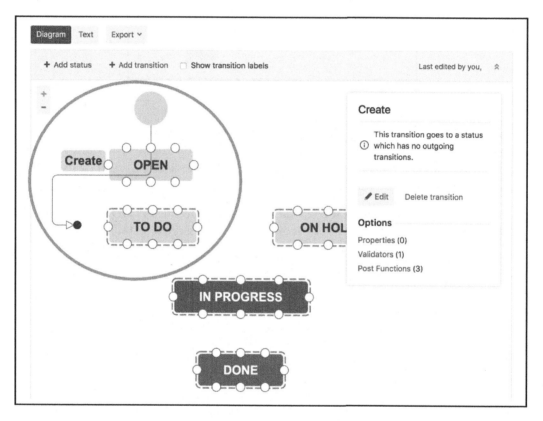

Figure 7

Now click on the **OPEN** status and, in the pop-up window, click on the **Remove status** link, as shown in the preceding screenshot. Finally, click on the **Remove** button in the **Confirm Remove Status** dialog box.

We now have the necessary statuses in our workflow. We need to create a transition between those statuses as per the requirements of our workflow.

First, click on the **TO DO** status, drag a line from this status to the **IN PROGRESS** status. A pop-up window called **Add Transition** will appear, shown as follows, where you will be asked to enter the **Name** of the transitions, which could be the same as your destination status or any name of your choosing:

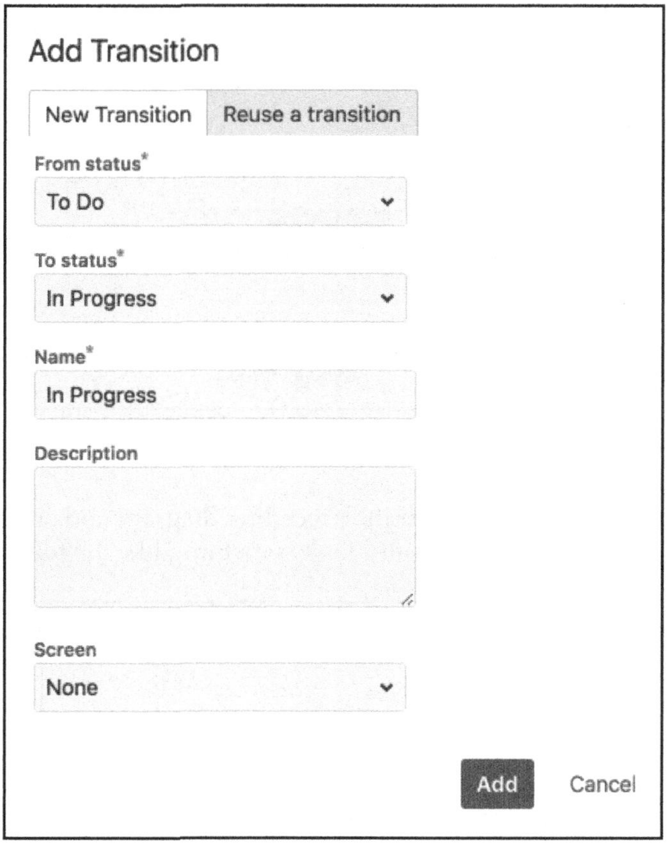

Add Transition

| New Transition | Reuse a transition |

From status*

To Do ⌄

To status*

In Progress ⌄

Name*

In Progress

Description

Screen

None ⌄

Add   Cancel

Figure 8

Remember that this transition name will appear to the end user when they work on the Jira issue. Click on the **Add** button to add a new transition.

The moment you add the transition, a line with an arrow representing a transition will be created between these two statues. The direction of the arrow is also important here. To add a transition back from **IN PROGRESS** to **TO DO,** you need to add one more transition, demonstrated as follows:

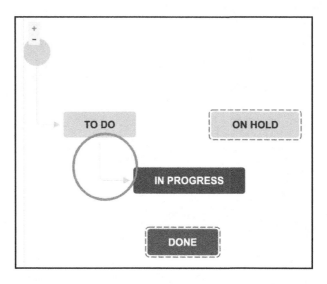

Figure 9

Now, refer to our proposed workflow in the preceding diagram and create the remainder of the transitions. Your final workflow should look something like the following diagram:

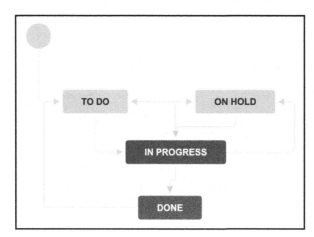

Figure 10

Our workflow is ready and all we need to do is use it in our project. We have just learned how to create a workflow, which is great, but there are lots of other customizations that can be done using workflow configurations, such as adding conditions and validators to our transitions.

Let's now go back to our project and use this workflow.

Go to **Project settings** | **Workflows** and then click on the **Add Workflow** button in the top-left corner, demonstrated as follows, and then click on the **Add Existing** option:

Figure 11

In the **Add Existing Workflow** popup, find the **Bug workflow** that you just created and click on the **Next** button, as follows:

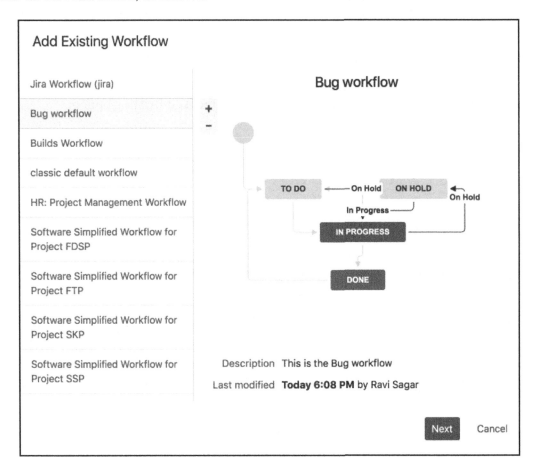

Figure 12

Then, in the **Assign Issue Types to "Bug workflow"** popup, select **Bug** and click on the **Finish** button, demonstrated as follows:

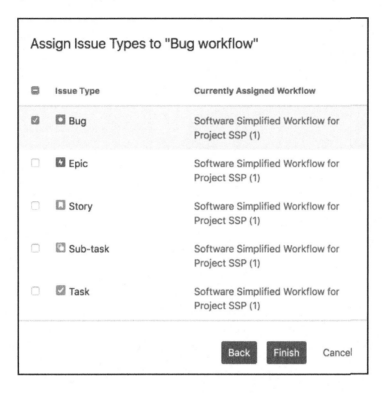

Figure 13

Finally, click on the **Publish** button at the top, demonstrated as follows:

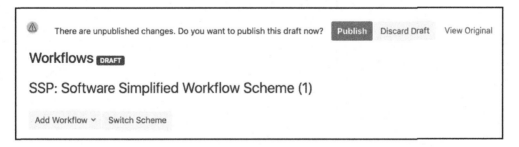

Figure 14

In the next set of screens, you may need to **Associate** any existing issue with the new workflow. Just follow the process and you will then have a new workflow in your existing workflow scheme for your project, shown as follows:

Figure 15

You can now see this new Bug workflow in action when you work on the bugs in your project. Just create a new issue of type bug in your project and you will notice that you now have a new workflow with custom transitions and statuses, demonstrated as follows:

Figure 16

By way of good practice, always check whether the new workflow is behaving as you expected.

Summary

Congratulations! You have now successfully started your journey of customizing Jira by creating your own workflow. In this chapter, we learned a lot, starting with an overview of various types of users in Jira and then we spent lot of time going through the process of creating a custom workflow and also using it in our existing project.

In the next chapter, we will continue customizing Jira further and take a look at how we can add more fields to our project by using screens and making sure that those new fields are visible only on a specific type of issue. We will also take a look at various permissions and learn how to modify them.

6
Configuring Project Screens and Permissions

In this chapter, we will continue customizing Jira further while take a look at how we can add more fields to our project by using screens and making sure that those new fields are visible only on a specific type of issue. We will also take a look at various permissions and learn how to modify them.

Topics covered in this chapter include the following:

- Adding new custom fields in Jira
- Understanding Jira screens
- Using the custom field in our project
- Transition screens
- Working with permissions

Adding new custom fields in Jira

In the previous chapter, we created a custom workflow that we want to use with the **Bug** issue type. We learned how to map this new workflow to the **Bug** issue type. This is great because the life cycle of the bug will be different compared to other issue types in Jira. However, we want to customize our project further; we want to capture additional information from the user who is reporting a bug. The additional information will be nothing but a new field in Jira, better known as a **Custom fields**.

Two new fields are required in our project: **Steps to reproduce** and **Type of Bug**. The first field will be a text field where the user can enter text freely, but the second field will be a drop-down from where user needs to select an item. Let's now add these two fields to our instance.

Perform the following steps to add a custom field:

1. In your Jira instance, go to **Jira settings** | **Issues** | **Custom fields** (under **FIELDS**)
2. Click on the **Add custom field** button in the top-right corner, demonstrated as follows:

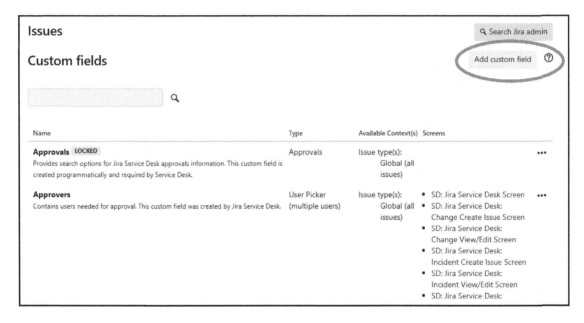

Figure 1

3. In the **Select a Field Type** popup, select **Text Field (multi-line)** and press the **Next** button, demonstrated as follows:

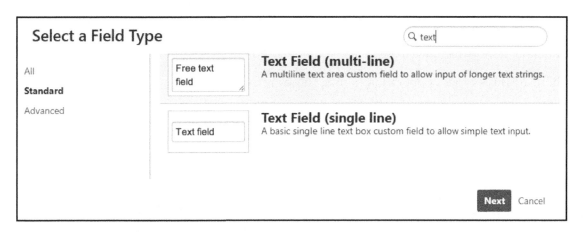

Figure 2

4. In the **Configure Text Field (multi-line) Field** pop up, enter the **Name** as Steps to reproduce and also add a meaningful **Description**. Finally, press the **Create** button.

Now, a custom field will be created in your instance of Jira. You will be asked to add this newly created custom field to a screen, but ignore this and continue with the creation of the field.

Follow the same set of instructions to add the Type of Bug custom field but, in this instance, the field type should be **Select List (single choice)** where you need to also add some **Options** for the user to select from the drop-down list.

Now that we have two new fields with us, let's now learn how to use them in our project.

Understanding Jira screens

Screens are nothing but containers of fields in Jira. Screens can have many fields in any order of your choosing. The order of the fields can be changed by you as well. Whenever you interact with an issue in Jira, you are, in most cases, working with a screen. To understand the screen, we have to also understand the concept of an operation.

There are three types of operation in Jira. These are as follows:

- Create issue
- Edit issue
- View issue

These operations are self-explanatory, but it is important to know here that the fields displayed on these operations can be different. When you create a new issue in Jira, you may just want to capture few fields, but when that issue is edited later, you may also want to capture more information. That is why these operations can have different screens associated with them.

In our case, we want the two new custom fields to be added in all three operations. In the next section, we will learn how to add the fields to our project.

Using the custom field in our project

Once you have added new custom fields to your instance, those fields are available globally for you to use in your project. Until you add those fields to your project, the fields will not be usable.

Perform the following steps to add the fields to the **Bug** issue type:

1. Inside your project, go to **Project settings | Screens.**

2. Under the **Screens** section, you will notice that there are two screen schemes already used in your project, as shown in the following screenshot. These two schemes are based on the template that we used earlier when we created the project:

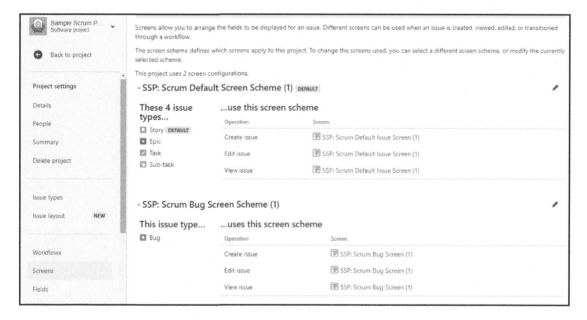

Figure 3

3. As you can see, there is a separate screen scheme used by the **Bug** issue type. Under this scheme, there is just one screen, called **SSP: Scrum Bug Screen (1)**, that is used by all three operations; in other words, **Create issue**, **Edit issue** and **View issue**.

4. To add our new fields, click on the screen **SSP: Scrum Bug Screen (1)** and, in the **Configure Screen** section, go to the bottom of the page were all the existing fields are listed, click on the **Select Field ...** drop-down, and select the two new fields that we added earlier, demonstrated as follows:

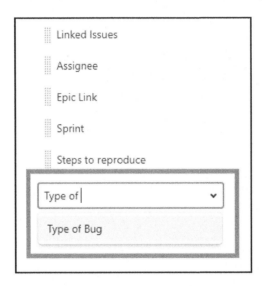

Figure 4

The fields will then be added to your project, but will only be available with the **Bug** issue type, as shown in the following screenshot:

Figure 5

You can also create your own screen scheme to map different screens to various operations because perhaps you don't want to capture a field during issue creation, but want to capture it later, when the issue is edited.

Transition screens

Apart from the screens used here, there is also the option to capture input from the user during workflow transitions, and this is done using transition screens.

What if we want the user to fill in a field called **Analysis** when the bug is resolved, but we do not want this field to be captured when we create a bug. In this case, we could create a new screen for the bug edit operation, but that would mean the user needs to click on the **Edit** button on the issue to enter information in this field. This requirement can be achieved by using a completely new screen and using that screen when the bug is resolved or, in our case, sent to **Done** status.

Perform the following steps to create a new screen and use it as a transition screen:

1. Firstly, create a new custom field as we did earlier in this chapter and name that field **Analysis**.
2. Now, go to **Jira settings** | **Issues** | **Screens** (under **SCREENS**) and click on the **Add screen** button in the top-right corner. In the **Add screen** popup, enter the **Name** as `Analysis screen` and a meaningful **Description,** as shown in the following screenshot:

Figure 6

3. Then, in the **Configure screen** section, add the **Analysis** field that you just created onto this screen.

4. Now, we need to use this screen containing just a single field in our Bug workflow. Go to **Project** | **Project settings** | **Workflows** and click on the pencil sign next to **Bug workflow** to edit it, as shown here:

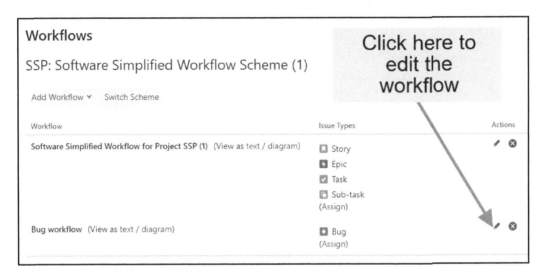

Figure 7

5. Now, inside your **Done** transition, click on the **Edit** button, as shown in the following screenshot:

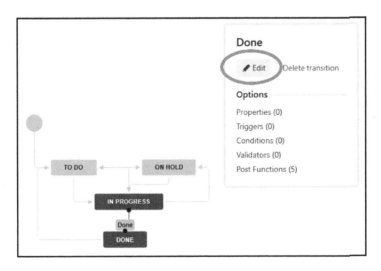

Figure 8

6. Then, in the **Edit Transition** popup, select **Screen** as **Analysis screen** and press the **Save** button, as shown in the following screenshot:

Figure 9

We are almost done now. After modifying the workflow, you also need to publish it, since this workflow was already attached to a project and used actively, hence, it needs to be published again. There will be a button at the top called **Publish Draft**. Press it to finally apply your changes to the project.

To test your new transition screen, go to any bug issue that you want to resolve by moving it to the **Done** state, as shown in the following screenshot:

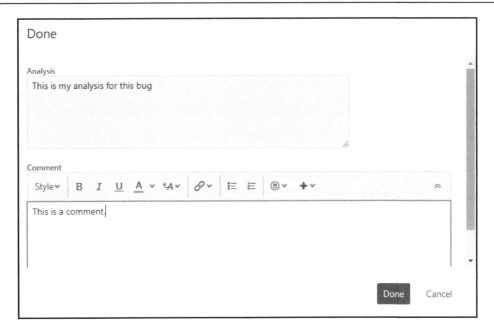

Figure 10

You will notice that a new screen will pop up, asking you to enter an analysis and a comment before finally changing the status of the bug to **Done**.

Working with permissions

We have implemented a significant number of customizations in our project. Now, let's take a look at one more configuration that will let you control who can do what in your project. Jira can be used by a small team comprising a few people to thousands of users in an enterprise and, with many people accessing a single instance, you may be worried about controlling your project permissions.

When you created the project earlier using a template, Jira created a number of default configurations and schemes, such as the issue type scheme, the workflow scheme, the issue type screen scheme, the permission scheme, and the notification scheme.

You can also create your own scheme with your own customized configurations. However, we can also use the configurations suggested by the template and later tweak them slightly. Let's now change the permissions for our project to hide it from everyone except people who have been added to our project by the project administrator.

In Jira, there is a concept of project role, which is nothing but a team of people or users per project. For example, there is a role called **Developers** in our instance where we can add more people. Now, what those people would do in that role depends really on the permissions defined in our permission scheme.

Perform the following steps to restrict access to our project to just a developer role:

1. First, we need to create a new permission scheme, so go to **Jira settings** ǀ **Issues** ǀ **Permission schemes** (under **ISSUE ATTRIBUTES**) and click on the **Copy** link under **Actions** for **Default Permission Scheme**.

2. Once the **Default Permission Scheme** is copied, then click on its **Edit** link under **Actions** and rename it to something else, such as **Software Permission Scheme**.

3. Now, we have a new permission scheme that we can modify. Click on the **Permissions** link of the new permission scheme and you will see lot of permissions related to project, comments, and who can do what, as shown in the following screenshot:

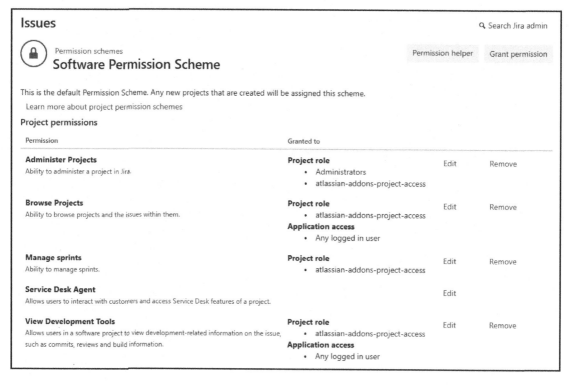

Figure 11

4. The second column, **Granted to**, has a list of either the individual user, group, or project role who have that permission.

5. To restrict access to a project, remove everything from the **Browse Projects** permission and only give it to **Project role developers**, as shown in the following screenshot:

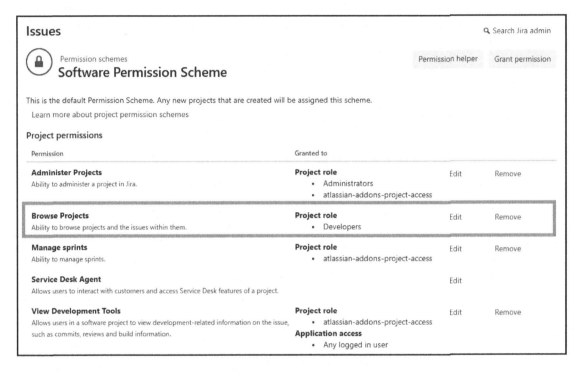

Figure 12

6. Now we have a new permission scheme that we can use in our project. In our project, go to **Project settings** | **Permissions** | **Actions** | **Use a different scheme**.

7. Now, select the **Scheme** that you just created and press the **Associate** button.

Congratulations! You have modified the permission scheme of your project and now, only people added to the **Developers** role in the project will have access to it.

Knowing how to perform these customizations will empower you to take control of your Jira instance and make it work for you the way you want. Jira out-of-the-box will come with a number of templates that you can always tweak further if you know the proper way to customize your instance.

Summary

In this chapter, we spent some time understanding how to add more custom fields from the users and also used them in our project by working on the screen. We also learned what transition screens are, and how they are different from normal screens. Finally, we modified the permissions of our project and restricted access to our project to a limited set of users. Although we only modified a single permission, knowing the right way to modify it is very important.

In the next chapter, we will look at the reporting capabilities of Jira. It is very important to know how to analyze the information that is already collected in our instance. Understanding how to track our progress using various reports and dashboards is a must-have skill that every Jira user and administrator ought to know.

7
Reports and Dashboards

In this chapter, we will look at the reporting capabilities of Jira. Once you start working on the project, you will also want to track the progress of your work and analyzing the information that you have in your instance is very important. It could be as simple as knowing how many issues are complete in order to create a graphical report.

Each project in Jira has its own set of reports that you can monitor from time to time. Depending upon the type of application you are using, the reports might vary slightly. We will also look at the dashboard, which is a great way to create our own custom reports.

Topics covered in this chapter include the following:

- Jira Core reports
- Jira Software reports
- Jira Service Desk
- Creating and sharing dashboards

Jira Core reports

In this book, we have looked at all three types of application in Jira. We began with Jira Core, which can be used by any business team in the company to track their day-to-day activities.

Let's first look at the in-built reports within a Jira Core-type project. To find these reports, go to the **Reports** section in your project sidebar and you will notice that here, the reports are grouped into three categories: **Issue analysis**, **Forecast & management**, and **Other**, as shown in the following screenshot:

Figure 1

Most of these reports are easy to configure and self-explanatory, but let's look at a number of key reports.

Average Age Report

The **Average Age Report** that follows shows the average age of unresolved issues for a project or filter. This helps you see whether your backlog is being kept up-to-date. Basically, it means the average number of days for which issues are in an unresolved state on a given date as follows:

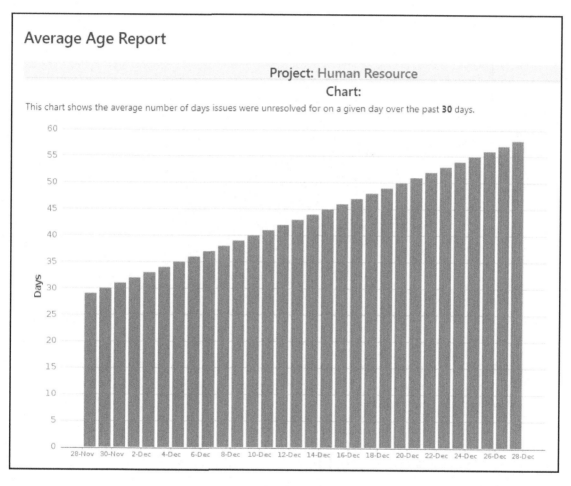

Figure 2

In this report, when you see that the bar is increasing over a period of time, this means that issues are not being resolved on time.

Pie Chart Report

This is one of the most useful reports, and shows the breakdown of issues based on various fields in Jira. For example, the following chart shows how issues are broken down based on their workflow status:

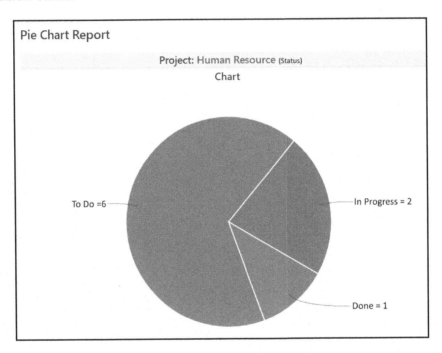

Figure 3

The preceding chart is telling us that there are lots of tasks still in the **To Do** state and action must be taken to improve this situation. Similar reports can be based on other Jira as well that are used in the project.

Jira Software reports

When you are working on an agile-based project, the reports that we saw earlier in the Jira Core section are also available here, but since Jira Software projects are different, you will also find a number of new reports here.

As demonstrated in the following diagram, you will find these reports under the **Agile** category within your **Reports** section:

Agile

Burndown Chart

Track the total work remaining and project the likelihood of achieving the sprint goal. This helps your team manage its progress and respond accordingly.

Burnup Chart

Track the total scope independently from the total work done. This helps your team manage its progress and better understand the effect of scope change.

Sprint Report

Understand the work completed or pushed back to the backlog in each sprint. This helps you determine if your team is overcommitting or if there is excessive scope creep.

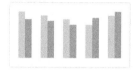

Velocity Chart

Track the amount of work completed from sprint to sprint. This helps you determine your team's velocity and estimate the work your team can realistically achieve in future sprints.

Cumulative Flow Diagram

Shows the statuses of issues over time. This helps you identify potential bottlenecks that need to be investigated.

Version Report

Track the projected release date for a version. This helps you monitor whether the version will release on time, so you can take action if work is falling behind.

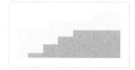

Epic Report

Understand the progress towards completing an epic over time. This helps you manage your team's progress by tracking the remaining incomplete/unestimated work.

Control Chart

Shows the cycle time for your product, version or sprint. This helps you identify whether data from the current process can be used to determine future performance.

Epic Burndown

Track the projected number of sprints required to complete the epic (optimized for Scrum). This helps you monitor whether the epic will release on time, so you can take action if work is falling behind.

Release Burndown

Track the projected release date for a version (optimized for Scrum). This helps you monitor whether the version will release on time, so you can take action if work is falling behind.

Figure 4

Let's now look at some important Agile-based reports.

Burndown chart

When we plan our sprint in a Jira Software scrum-based project, we have the option to estimate our work using either story points or the number of hours. The following report shows the progress of the issues in a specific sprint based on the total estimated effort versus the actual effort:

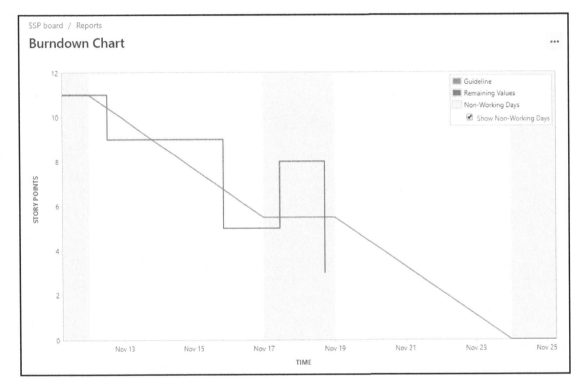

Figure 5

If you look at the preceding chart, you will notice that in the beginning, the total story points planned were 11 and, based on the sprint duration, ideally, the total story points should be burned by the end of the sprint. This is represented by the baseline going down. As the work begins, another line representing the actual completion of the work will start that follows the original baseline. In an ideal scenario, the actual line should follow the baseline and, if the line goes up, then this means that more work is added in between the sprint, which is not good practice.

If the gap between the actual line and the baseline is too great, this means that it is unlikely that the team will complete its work on time.

A burndown chart is one of the most important reports in Agile-based projects that follow SCRUM.

Velocity chart

Another important report that we will discuss is the velocity chart, which actually talks about the capacity of the team. Let's first look at the report, illustrated as follows:

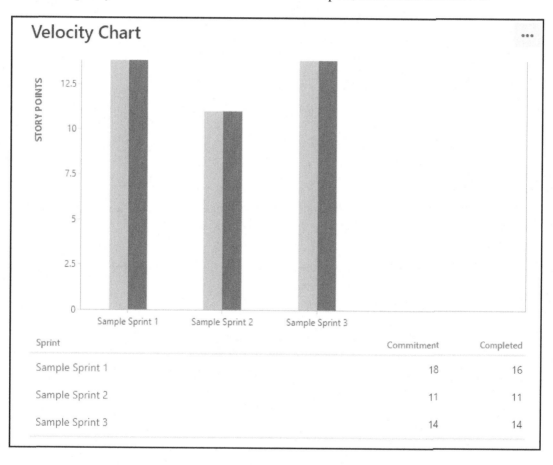

Sprint	Commitment	Completed
Sample Sprint 1	18	16
Sample Sprint 2	11	11
Sample Sprint 3	14	14

Figure 6

When the sprint is planned, an estimation is done regarding the work that can probably be finished by the end of the sprint. At the start of a new project, this is a little difficult to estimate. Also, as the project progresses, team members might change or become unavailable, so it is very important to know the current capacity of the team.

The preceding chart tells us that in **Sample Sprint 1**, the team's commitment was **18**, but **16** completed, while in **Sample Sprint 2**, the team's commitment was **11**, and **11** completed, and finally, in **Sample Sprint 3**, the commitment was also delivered and completed.

Hence, the average capacity of the team is 16+11+14 divided by 3, in other words, 13.6, or roughly 14. Hence, based on past performance, we can allocate work to this team worth 14 story points.

This information is crucial for the manager because, if this number is too low or dropping, then appropriate action can be taken on time to improve it.

Jira Service Desk

Let's now look at some important Jira Service Desk reports that are unique to Service Desk only.

SLA success rate

One of the unique features of Jira Service Desk is the concept of **service-level agreements** (**SLAs**) that you can configure for your project. Let's look at the following report concerning two SLAs:

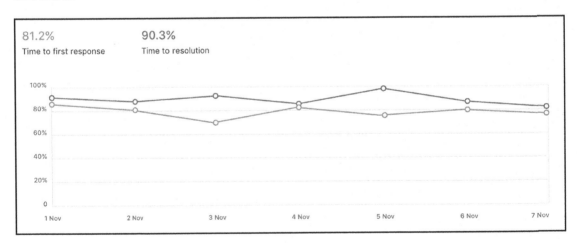

Figure 7

This report provides the success rate percentage for the two SLAs that we have in the project—**Time to first response** and **Time to resolution**. There is a trend line as well that shows this information over time.

Satisfaction

In Jira Service Desk, there is an in-built feature that will ask the customers to provide their feedback. This is extremely important for the team, as this will tell them whether their service is good or bad. Let's look at the report first:

Figure 8

This report is telling us an **Average rating** on a scale of one to five stars and is quite detailed. You can see the customer **Comment**, the issue **Key**, and also the **Agent** who was involved in the resolution of the ticket.

Creating and sharing dashboards

The reports we discussed earlier in this chapter are project specific and available when you are within a project. However, when you log in to your Jira instance, the first thing you see is a system dashboard, which is a default dashboard containing a set of small reports also known as gadgets. We can always create our own custom dashboard showing us information from one or multiple projects.

One advantage of the dashboard is that you don't need to go to individual projects and configure various reports one by one. Using the dashboard, you can get a bird's-eye view of what is happening in your project or team in one go. Let's create our own dashboard.

On the **System dashboard**, click on the three dots in the top-right corner and select **Create dashboard**, demonstrated as follows:

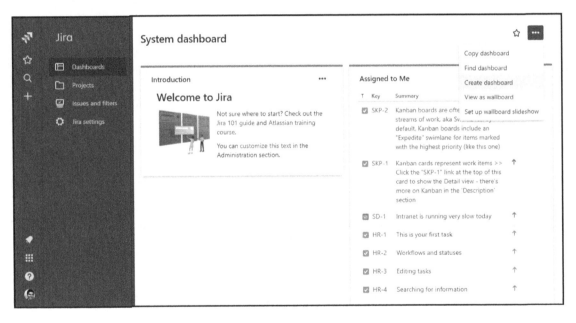

Figure 9

Enter the **Name** and **Description**, select with whom you want to share it, and then click on the **Create** button, demonstrated as follows:

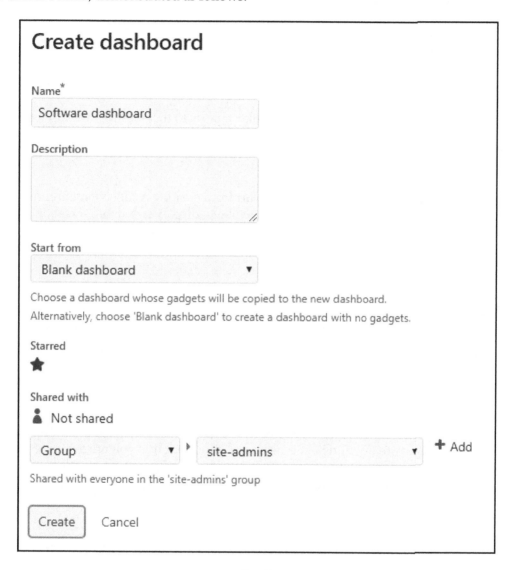

Figure 10

You will then have an empty dashboard with the option to add various gadgets. Let's add the following gadgets to our dashboard:

- **Average Age Chart**
- **Sprint Burndown Gadget**
- **Pie Chart: Sample Scrum Project**
- **Agile Wallboard Gadget**

Yes, you have guessed correctly. These are similar reports to the ones that we discussed earlier, but this time, we want to have them handy on our dashboard. The gadgets will let you choose the project for which you want to create a report. Once you do that, your dashboard will be ready.

One great thing about the dashboard is that, apart from creating a collection of reports in a single place, you can share it with other team members, display it on a big screen in your office, and, most importantly, you can create multiple dashboards showing different information from a variety of projects.

Summary

In this chapter, we learned how to analyze the information that we already have in our Jira instance by first looking at various reports that come out-of-the-box, and later, we configured our own custom dashboard to have all those reports available to hand in one place.

In the next and final chapter, we will discuss best practices that you should always keep in mind when using Jira, and also when you are customizing the tool because, although Jira allows you to configure many things, it is also very important that you are aware of the consequences if these customizations are not done right. Observing best practices will ensure the longevity and top-notch performance of your Jira instance.

8
Best Practices

In this, the final chapter, we will focus on a number of best practices that you should always keep in mind when using Jira. You must have already realized that Jira is quite a flexible tool when it comes to customizing it, based on your requirements. At the same time, it is very important that configuration changes in Jira are done carefully from the outset and that you are aware of the consequences if these customizations are not performed correctly. Observing best practices will ensure the longevity and top-notch performance of your Jira instance.

Topics covered in this chapter include the following:

- Setting up a change control board
- Documenting your configurations
- Not creating too many statuses
- Not creating lots of custom fields
- Using contexts
- Using project roles over groups
- Not modifying default configurations
- Jira customization process

Setting up a change control board

If your organization has just started using Jira, or wants to use it, then the very first thing that should be done is to set up some sort of change control board. Jira can be installed easily at the outset for piloting and, especially if you are planning to use Jira Cloud, then it literally takes minutes to set up a new instance and you can start using it straight away, mainly because Jira comes with project templates. However, as the number of teams expands and Jira is adopted by many of them, the majority will ask the administrator to modify the projects slightly based on their requirements.

Since Jira is quite easy to modify, it might be tempting to just implement the new changes straight away, and this is what we want to warn you about. Treat Jira like any other project and, in the beginning, create a standard set of configurations that can be used by a wide range of teams. Although Jira administrators are responsible for the tool, they should also advocate the standardization of various processes. For example, if there are two teams working in the same company on a similar project, then ideally, they both should be using the same configurations in Jira.

The purpose of the change control board is to ensure that, on an ongoing basis, the Jira customizations are done by first reviewing the changes, challenging the team, and advising them on using standard configurations.

Documenting your configurations

The worst nightmare of Jira administrators is a Jira instance with hundreds of workflows and other customizations without any idea of their purpose. Jira instances can grow big very quickly in an enterprise setup and that is why it is absolutely imperative that the configurations executed in the tool from the very outset are documented in detail. It may seem cumbersome, but once it is done from the very beginning, it helps the Jira administrators a lot in maintaining the instance. You need to ensure that, with every customization undertaken in the tool, and not just at the start but on an ongoing basis as well, the document is also updated.

Documenting is important because, when a new person joins the team of Jira administrators, they can always refer to the documentation to understand the purpose of the configuration. This document should ideally contain the purpose of the configuration, target project types, actual configurations, and feedback from the stakeholders or your users.

Not creating too many statuses

Workflows are one of the main aspects of Jira customizations. They define the life cycle of an issue as it goes through different stages. A workflow has a variety of statuses, and various transitions between them. Sometimes, when a new workflow is created, there might be a requirement to create a new status. Now, before creating a new status, please go through the existing list of statues in your instance and check whether any of those existing statuses can be reused.

Reusing a status is only possible when their names are a bit generic and not overly project-specific. For example, **Awaiting feedback** and **Feedback awaited** are more or less the same, and there is no need to create a status such as **Feedback 123**.

Statuses are created globally and Jira workflows can use them, which is why you should not try to create too many statuses.

Not creating lots of custom fields

Earlier in this book, we learned how to create custom fields. The purpose of these fields is to store some additional information that is otherwise not possible with default system fields in Jira.

Too many custom fields is the biggest reason for slow performance in Jira. There really is no reason to have hundreds of custom fields in Jira and caution should be exercised when creating a new custom field. Just as with statuses, try to reuse a custom field and also try to create custom fields with generic names.

Let's take a look at some generic custom fields that can be created in Jira instances:

Custom field	Type	Description
Client/customer	Select List	This uses Project Context to create different options for multiple projects
Category	Select List	Labels and components should be used in most cases, but this generic field can be used in many projects with different options using Project Context
External ID	Text Field	This field will be used to store the ID of the issue, which is stored in an external tool
Type of testing	Select List	This field can be used when Jira is used for test management
Start date	Date Picker	Jira does come with a due date, but the start date of a task is not available

As you can see in the preceding table, the idea is to optimize field utilization. Since these fields store information for every project and issues therein, the performance of the instance can be degraded if there are lots of fields.

Using contexts

In the previous section, we discussed optimizing the use of custom fields, but sometimes, the same custom field requires a different set of options for each project. For example, a field such as **Customer name** can have different options based on the team or project, and w e are talking about a **Select List** type of field.

In such scenarios, we highly recommend that you use custom field contexts that will let you create different sets of options based on the project, but where the fields remain the same.

Using project roles over groups

Maintaining a Jira instance, especially in a growing organization, can be a daunting task. There are a number of activities that can only be done by Jira administrators, so you should ensure that project administrators are also able to manage their projects as much as they can. This is especially true when more people are added to the project. There are many configurations, such as permissions, notifications, and workflows, that are based on users. When creating these configurations, if you use a Jira group instead of project roles, then your project administrators are dependent on you to add/remove people, but they do have permissions to manage their own team of users using project roles.

Not modifying default configurations

Jira comes with a lot of templates and default configurations, as you may have seen earlier. These configurations help you get started with Jira quickly but, as a good practice, you should never modify them directly. If you want to use any of the default configurations, feel free to copy them and then modify the copied version.

Jira customization process

Finally, let's summarize the customization process that you can employ to kick-start the use of Jira in your organization. It is based on the best practices that we discussed earlier.

You can perform these steps to begin the customization process:

1. Pilot Jira with default configurations
2. Gather feedback
3. Document the proposed configurations
4. Test the configurations in a sandbox
5. Implement them in production
6. Standardize the configurations
7. Set up a change control board

The preceding mentioned steps are self-explanatory, and we have already covered them either in this chapter or earlier in this book.

Summary

In this chapter, we looked at various best practices that you must employ in your organization when implementing Jira. The purpose of them is to not only ensure good performance of your instance, but to also ensure that administration of the instance does not become more difficult over time.

This was the final chapter in this book. Their purpose of this book was to get you started on Jira cloud instance quickly with a view to using them in your organization, but we also covered the customization aspects of Jira. We hope this book will empower you to start using Jira with confidence and we wish you all the best on your journey.

Other Books You May Enjoy

If you enjoyed this book, you may be interested in these other books by Packt:

Hands-On Agile Software Development with JIRA
David Harned

ISBN: 9781789532135

- Create your first project (and manage existing projects) in JIRA
- Manage your board view and backlogs in JIRA
- Run a Scrum Sprint project in JIRA
- Create reports (including topic-based reports)
- Forecast using versions
- Search for issues with JIRA Query Language (JQL)
- Execute bulk changes to issues
- Create custom filters, dashboards, and widgets
- Create epics, stories, bugs, and tasks

Selenium WebDriver Quick Start Guide
Pinakin Chaubal

ISBN: 9781789612486

- Understand what an XPath is and how to design a customized XPath
- Learn how to create a Maven project and build
- Create a Singleton driver
- Get to grips with Jenkins integration
- Create a factory for browsers
- Implement multi-browser testing with Selenium Grid
- Create a sample pop-up window and JavaScript alert
- Report using Extent Reports

Leave a review - let other readers know what you think

Please share your thoughts on this book with others by leaving a review on the site that you bought it from. If you purchased the book from Amazon, please leave us an honest review on this book's Amazon page. This is vital so that other potential readers can see and use your unbiased opinion to make purchasing decisions, we can understand what our customers think about our products, and our authors can see your feedback on the title that they have worked with Packt to create. It will only take a few minutes of your time, but is valuable to other potential customers, our authors, and Packt. Thank you!

Index

W

Work in Progress (WIP) 45